Presented To

_____

Presented By

_____

Date

_____

Daughters of Heaven®
Devotional

An Interactive Devotional for God's Girls

by

Suzanne Rentz

Harrison House
Tulsa, OK

10 09 08 07 06   10 9 8 7 6 5 4 3 2

Daughters of Heaven® *Devotional—*
An Interactive Devotional for God's Girls
ISBN 1-57794-799-1
Copyright © 2003 by Suzanne Rentz
8319 Cedar Crest Way
Sacramento, CA 95826
www.daughtersofheaven.org

Published by Harrison House, Inc.
P.O. Box 35035
Tulsa, Oklahoma 74153

Contents

Created for Such a Time As This

Endnotes

Introduction

What an opportunity for adventure we all are given from the moment our tiny baby-sized lungs fill with oxygen for the first time to the instant we release our last breath. Life—it is precious; it is purposed. Jeremiah 29:11 records our Creator's intentions, His "travel" plans for our lives:

> For I know the plans I have for you…plans to prosper you and not to harm you, plans to give you hope and a future.

This familiar verse resounds with the commitment that our heavenly Father has made to us and is an underlying message throughout this devotional. God has created each of us with a specific purpose. There isn't a living, breathing human being walking around on this planet that God hasn't purposed to be here.

But for so many young women, discovering our purpose, our true worth, our value and identity, and becoming a true woman of God seems to be more of a dream than a reality. We experience a continual struggle to achieve godliness in an ungodly world. Society tries to dictate our appearance, our morals, and our individual sense of value and self-worth.

We don't have to be conformed any longer to the patterns of the world. There is a better way—God's way. He even tells us that in His Word: "Don't copy the behavior and customs of this world, but let God transform you into a new person by changing the way you think. Then you will know what God wants you to do, and you will know how good and pleasing and perfect his will really is" (Rom. 12:2 NLT).

You see, God's destination for your life has been planned, but the journey is based upon the decisions you make along the way. This devotional was written to encourage you to make the most of your most awesome, valuable possession—your life. In these pages I hope to inspire, instruct, and challenge you to pursue and fulfill the wonderful plan and purpose God has just for you. (See Eph. 2:10.) Each entry is designed to equip you with life-changing truths about important issues you face daily to help you make the right choices.

Throughout your life you will be forced to make many life and death decisions. You may need to make the right choice about dating and sexuality, about abortion, about your appearance (especially relating to eating disorders), to name a few. The purpose of this book is to help you to know that when you come face to face with an obstacle, and you will, you can avoid the roadblocks and pitfalls and take the right route. If you use poor judgment and steer off course, you can repent and get back on the road. And always remember that as you are on this journey, God is there with you, holding your hand every step of the way. (See Isa. 41:13.)

No Limits

It has been said that people tend to support what they help to create. That means that when people feel a part of something, they will give it all they've got. They will stay committed to the cause. Know that God, your Creator, will always stay committed to you; He is committed to your cause. I pray that you will invest in your relationship with Him—study His Word, learn His voice, and know His heart. Stay close to Him, because the course He has charted for you is a magnificent one that you won't want to miss.

There's no limit to what God can do in and through your life when you have a relationship with Him.

Oh yes, and always remember that when fear, doubt, struggle, uncertainty, or pain come your way, you don't hold your destiny in your own hand. You can look to the One who does.

> Trust in the Lord with all your heart and lean not on your own understanding;
> In all your ways acknowledge Him and He will make your paths straight.
>
> Proverbs 3:5,6

The Heart of the Father

I talk very well in front of my sons about their father, but I don't make him out to be some incredible superhero. Yet they know that he's strong and big and smart, because they have experienced his strength and his wisdom for themselves.

He sometimes wrestles with them, and at bedtime he often carries all of them upstairs at the same time. When they go through a tough time, he has good advice for them. He's got a hug and a kiss for them every night. He spends time with them. So they not only know their dad, but they've experienced an intimate, father-son relationship with him; they know how much he loves them.

Do you know that God, our heavenly Father, longs for us to know Him and how much He loves us? If we can ever really grasp the truth about who our Father is and the depth of His love for us, I believe that it will be the bridge that connects us to God, that takes head knowledge (knowing about God) and applies it to the heart (knowing Him intimately).

Seeing Through a Filter

One morning I went to the grocery store to buy some bread. When I walked into the store, I was clueless that I was still wearing my sunglasses (which have yellowish-tint lenses). As I walked down the bread aisle, I couldn't find the usual brand that I buy. It came in a green bag, and I began to get frustrated because I was in a hurry and all I could find were blue-colored bags.

There wasn't a green package anywhere in sight, so I bent down to pick up the blue package. As I did, it dawned on me that the package looked blue because I was wearing my sunglasses. The tint in my lenses had changed my perception of the color of the package.

Now, you're probably wondering why in the world I am talking about bread. But there is a point to this story. It illustrates the fact that we can have a warped perception of God, which often comes from our experiences with other people and circumstances.

The bread was right in front of me, and yet I didn't see it for what it was because the tint in my sunglasses had changed the truth and the reality of it for me. That is sometimes the way we see ourselves, the way we see our future, our life. But most importantly, that is often the way we see God—through "tinted lenses," or what I call a filter. The truth or reality might be directly in front of us, and yet we can't see it. When we see through a "filter," things that should make sense sometimes just don't.

Do you see God through some kind of filter? The revelation of His unconditional love and acceptance of you is life-changing. So right now we're going to look at some filters that can affect how we see God and learn about His heart toward us as our heavenly Father.

The Legalistic, Authoritarian Filter

Our relationship with our earthly father can create a filter. My husband, Mark, had a wonderful father when he was growing up. His dad was handsome, had a successful business, and had many great qualities. But his dad was a perfectionist; he expected a lot from himself and others. He was a good man and a very good father, but at times he was really hard on his children.

For example, when it was Mark's turn to do dishes, if he didn't thoroughly wash them and his dad found a little tiny bit of food on them, his dad would have him do dishes that entire week. So he had to make sure those dishes were perfectly clean. It was the same rule for his brother and sister.

When Mark became a Christian, he loved God, and he understood about fearing or reverencing God, about His holiness and our need to be saved. But Mark wrestled with the fact that God was full of grace and unconditional acceptance toward him. It was easier for Mark to relate to not measuring up and to see God as legalistic and authoritarian. Mark described it to me one time, comparing it to the way our two oldest sons learned to ride a bike.

Luke, my oldest, is a thinker; he has to analyze the situation. When he got on a bike for the first time, he was really wobbly because he was thinking, *Am I going to ride in that crack in the sidewalk?* and *Okay, how much do I have to turn the handlebars to make the turn?* He didn't go very fast, so he'd wobble a lot. It took him a long time to just relax and enjoy riding his bike because he was so afraid of falling off or crashing into something.

Andrew is just the opposite. When he got on the bike, Mark couldn't even keep up with him. He rode fast and enjoyed it right from the beginning. If he'd fall, he'd just get back up, laughing, and start riding again.

Mark's understanding of God was similar to the way Luke initially rode a bike. Mark was concentrating on failing, on falling, on his sin nature, more than he was on enjoying the "ride" of life. God wants us to experience life abundantly. He wanted Mark to enjoy his life and relationship with his heavenly Father. But Mark saw God through a filter that developed from some of his experiences with his earthly father. It affected him until he began to realize, *Wait a minute, I'm missing out on a whole big part of God.*

The Divorce Filter

Divorce is another filter that distorts how we see God. In the beginning your life may be rolling along, smooth, steady, secure in the solid foundation of your family, and things are intact. Then all of a sudden your life is turned upside down because your parents are divorcing. Now everything that you thought was up is down. You don't know your left from your right. What was your security has suddenly, completely crumbled.

I have a friend whose parents got a divorce when she was a child. One time I asked her to describe what she felt from that experience, and she shared, "I felt this incredible, deep sadness. There were times when I felt like it was my fault, maybe if I hadn't been born, maybe I was just in the way." She had nothing to do with the divorce, yet that is not an uncommon feeling among children from divorced families.

As children, we take in what's happening and apply it to our lives, and often we get all confused. My friend felt an incredible sadness; then there was anger, and then she was mad. She's just recently come to the place where she's feeling stronger and more secure.

When you experience a divorce, it can become a filter that causes you to wonder, *God, are You upside down just like the rest of my world? You know, I heard about You, and I heard that You were my Rock. What's going on, God? My family life and everything I knew has crumbled. Have You left me, too?*

If that describes how you feel, remember that your life may change, but Jesus never changes (Heb. 13:8), and He said, "...I will never leave you nor forsake you" (Heb. 13:5).

The No-time Dad Filter

Some good friends of mine have four children. When an opportunity arose for them to pastor a small church, they were so excited;

they thought it was going to be an awesome experience. They had big plans, big dreams, and some very contemporary ideas.

As soon as they arrived, some of the congregation began to gossip, complain, and backbite. When my friends wanted to start making their changes, many of those people left the church. It became so bad that the church membership went down, which caused the church income to go down, and my friends had to take on additional jobs to have enough income to support their family.

One of their sons had a hard time accepting all that was happening. He wanted to spend time with his dad, but his dad was drained; his dad was crushed and burned out from working so much, and he had no time or energy left for his son. That young man had to sit there and watch it all. Maybe you have a dad in ministry, or maybe your dad just works a lot so he's not around, and you can relate to this situation.

Their son was a teenager, and he began making some bad choices. Soon his mom got a call from the police department—he had been caught driving under the influence of alcohol.

He had started looking at God through a filter saying, "You know what? All You do is take. You take my dad's joy and his peace. God, You just want to use him and spit him out. I'm not going to serve You." It affected the way he saw God. He was resentful, and it got in the way of his relationship with God. He couldn't see his Father God for who He is.

The Absentee Father Filter

It is so common for children to be raised without a dad. In fact, two of my best friends were raised that way. One of them told me that when she was little, her dad left. She never had him around for any of the firsts—the first time she took a step, her first day of school, her first date, the day she graduated from high school. Her dad was nowhere to be seen, and she always felt as if he could care less about her.

After she became a Christian, she wanted to be in ministry, so she went to Bible school where she earned a degree and later became a children's pastor. But there was a big part of her that was not fulfilled because her concept of God was affected by her earthly dad's rejection of her. She wondered how in the world could God accept her if her own earthly father didn't. She struggled with feelings of insecurity because she always felt second or third best. She wrestled with the idea of God's complete love for her.

The Sexual Abuse Filter

When you've been molested, especially by your earthly father, you take on the shame of it all. It may cause you to see God through a filter of shame, and you may feel dirty no matter what you do. If you are presently in an abusive situation (sexual or physical), seek help immediately. Talk to your youth pastor, school guidance counselor, or a trusted teacher or friend. Or look in the yellow pages or on an Internet Web site for a teen organization that offers help. The point is, get help now!

And remember that although you may think you've hidden it, that no one knows, God knows, and you need to talk to Him about it, too. You need to let it out. You need to ask God to fill you up with His power, His love, His peace and joy. He can help you and enable you to experience a feeling of purity.

Acceptance Brings Peace

We may not realize it, but seeing God through these different kinds of filters can become a part of our everyday thoughts and pattern of living. They can cause us to miss out on totally experiencing an intimate, loving relationship with the Lord. That's why it's so important to become at peace in your situation with your earthly dad.

I had a wonderful dad. My dad was awesome. He wasn't perfect; he didn't go around the house saying, "I love you, Suzanne," and hugging me all the time. But he was always there for me. And I knew I could count on that from him. At all of my singing recitals, at every tap dance and ballet recital, at everything I did, he was always in the audience just watching me, proud of me.

I wanted so much to spend time with my dad. I can remember how he would read at night when I was a child, and I'd just go cuddle up next to him, put my head on his chest, and feel so secure. When I was in high school, I felt that I wanted to spend more time with him. So I started getting up early and going out to breakfast with him. It was our little time together, and it was so special; we continued doing that even after I finished high school.

Then one day when I was twenty-one, I received a phone call that my dad had been killed in a car crash. It was devastating. I cried for days, and I kept thinking, *How am I going to get over this? I love my dad so much.* But with God's help, I did make it through that difficult time. And I was so glad that I had been at peace with my dad and had been able to spend so many special times with him.

You never know how long you're going to have with someone you love. It's important to understand that you can be at peace with your earthly father, whether or not he's been a part of your life.

Number one, communicate how you feel. It seems that as teenagers, we often feel as if we've got to harden our hearts and be rebellious with our fathers instead of just telling them how we feel. If your dad's too busy or you're struggling to take the first step in building your relationship and communicate, just start; let him know how you feel. Don't keep it inside. Maybe you don't know your father; maybe he's not in your life anymore, and you don't know where he is. Find someone you trust and talk to them about your feelings for your dad.

Number two, learn to forgive when there's a problem. In Proverbs 4:23 the Bible talks about guarding your heart "for it is the wellspring of life." What is a wellspring? In a kingdom that had a castle, the most secure, fortified place in the castle was the wellspring. They had it guarded up, boarded up, and no one could get to it because if the enemy could get to the wellspring and poison it, the entire kingdom would be destroyed.

That wellspring was more important than the walls around the castle. It was crucial. And you know what? We have an enemy called Satan who wants to get to our heart and poison it with negative thoughts and feelings and destroy our life. That's why we need to guard our heart.

One of the best things you can do is to guard it from unforgiveness because that turns to resentment, which will destroy your life. Unforgiveness will be discussed later on, but for now know that you need to learn to forgive (not only others, but yourself as well), because after you've communicated how you feel and after you've forgiven them, it doesn't matter what they do anymore; you forgive them regardless. If they continue on, you just release it, and let it go.

Number three, learn to accept instead of expect. Only one Dad will ever be perfect and that is your heavenly Father. If I had wanted my dad to be a dad who hugged me and kissed me and said I was the best every waking moment, I would have constantly been disappointed.

I remember talking to an older lady about her dad. At the end of the conversation, after she told me some horrible things about him, I tried to explain about personality differences, about the way they show their love, and how sometimes we can misunderstand each other. At the end of the conversation I asked her, "If your dad doesn't change, are you willing to accept your relationship the way it is now?"

She told me that she'd have to think about it, and soon after, I found out that she chose not to have a relationship with her father. I felt so bad for her because she was willing to trade what could have been so wonderful for nothing at all.

The bottom line is, learn to accept who your dad is. I think sometimes we expect way too little. Rise up to the occasion; take it as a challenge. Get on a mission to find something you can share with your dad, if that is possible. Learn to forgive, learn to communicate and treasure your time with your dad. Treasure it, hold it dear to you. Make the most of it; make the most of your relationship and be at peace.

It's possible that you might not ever be able to completely reconcile with your earthly father. Maybe you never knew him. But you can still be at peace about it; you can look at all the good that you have, and you can let go of the bad. That is an important choice only you can make, because when you are at peace is when you can experience an intimate, loving relationship with your heavenly Father.

The Father's Heart

God cherishes His daughters. That is His heart toward you; your Father God loves you so much. Did you know that you are perfect in His sight, that you are a masterpiece to Him? Part of my personality is that I become excited when something turns out good; I'm all fired up. Well, do you know that God took so much time and care in creating you, that when you were born, He was fired up over you?

My little boys actually think that heaven had a big party with balloons and streamers when they were born. They are firmly convinced that the angels were dancing and singing the day of their birth. I believe that, too! In fact, the day you were born, I can just imagine God looking at you and making loving comments: "Look at my little girl. She's beautiful. Would you look at that nose? Look at her little fingers and her little toes."

Usually we focus so much on the outside, but God is more interested in our heart and our life than in our outward appearance. He wasn't fired up just about your physical appearance. When God molded you and formed you, He also put dreams inside of you, dreams yet to be fulfilled. He put desires in you. He created you so perfect in His eyes.

I want to tell you something that may surprise you—God *likes* you. That may sound strange, because we're so used to hearing that God *loves* us. He not only loves you; He *likes* you! You are cool to God!

Recently, I had to get a picture taken for a brochure. So I went to a photographer, posed, and took two pictures. Afterward, he said to me, "Do you know we can change the background?" I said, "Maybe if I get the right kind of background, it will be better." So we started looking at his selections.

Then I suggested to him that if we could change the background, maybe we could smooth out the wrinkles on my face. He agreed and smoothed out my wrinkles in the photograph. When I saw how great that looked, I said, "My teeth don't look very white. Is there anything we can do to whiten them a little bit?" He answered, "Piece of cake," and proceeded to whiten my teeth in the picture. But they looked a little too white to me, so he had to tint them.

It seemed as if I kept finding more flaws in my picture. After he improved the look of my teeth, I said to him, "My teeth look so white now, what about fixing my eyes? They look as if they're set in a little deep. Is there anything we can do about that?"

This went on for quite some time. We finally stopped touching up the photo when I asked him to give me highlights in my hair, which made me look as if I had fuzzy skunk hair.

What had happened? The more I stared at my picture and tried to change it, the more I didn't like it, and the more I saw my flaws. The more I sat there and tried to change and perfect myself, the more I realized, *I can't believe all the flaws I have.* To this day, it's hard for me to look at that picture because I see flaws in my appearance.

What an illustration of the way we often look at our own lives. When we don't look at our lives through God's eyes, we try and perfect what we think are flaws in ourselves. The truth is that your Father God created you, and in His eyes you are perfect. Remember, He not only loves you, He likes you.

Unlike the no-time dad, God desires to walk with you; He desires to be a part of your life. If you sang for the first time in front of a group of people, He was right there in the background saying, "That's My girl." If you were in a swim meet and you took second place, He said, "I know you could have gotten first, but I'm proud of second." If your friend betrayed you, and you were so crushed and so broken, your Father God saw that, and He hurt for you. If you faced a huge disappointment, your Father God was there, too.

One of the aspects about God that I love so much is that He is El Roi, "...the God who sees..." (Gen. 16:13). He's the God who knows everything, and He still loves us so intimately. He desires that we walk in His Presence and that we communicate with Him. He's not interested in rhyming prayers or hearing us use big, religious-sounding words when we pray. He wants the truth; He wants reality. He wants us to tell Him what's going on and how we feel.

There are times when I'm upset, and I tell Him the whole situation. But there are times that I am so overwhelmed with how awesome He is that my eyes fill with tears as I begin to feel His Presence.

Do you know what else? There are times when I am scared to death about things, but I've learned to stretch out my hand at those times and say, "Father God, hold my hand and walk me through this. I can't make it without You, but with You, I can do all things" (Phil. 4:13), and He helps me. It's just like a little girl with so many things all over her room that she can't see the way to walk out of there. Then her dad comes in, takes her by the hand, and says, "Come on, I'll guide you through this."

Every time I feel insecure, every time I face a scary situation, every time circumstances seem to be out of control, I am holding His hand. And the best part is that I know He's holding me.

… He gathers the lambs in his arms and carries them close to his heart….

Isaiah 40:11

Sheltered by the Rock

Our Father God not only carries us, but He is our Rock. When our world is shaken, He is still our Rock; He is our Foundation. Psalm 91 describes God as being our shelter. That means you can run to Him, and He is there for you. When you face huge disappointments, when people fail you, because they will, and when circumstances are so out of control, and they will be at times, when it's foggy, and you can't see where to step next, the one thing you can be sure of is that your Father God will remain unchanged. He will always be your firm Foundation, your strong Tower, your Refuge from the storms of life. If you remember nothing else, remember that you can always put your feet on the Foundation (of His Word), and you will not fall; you will not stumble.

Sometimes I think we give up on ourselves. We think, *I have failed one too many times, and I am not going to repent anymore because I'll probably fail again.* You know what? Your heavenly Father believes in you when you don't believe in yourself, when you can't believe in yourself, when you think you've lost it all. He's right there saying, "I believe in you. Let's do it again. Let's try again." He'll never give up on you. He'll always be there believing in you, knowing that you can make it with His help.

My husband and I have three awesome sons. But we are considering adopting a little girl. If we do adopt one, she's going to be part of our family. She's going to have the Rentz name, and everything that Mark and I have will be hers. I believe she will take on our nature as her parents, that she will take on a new identity. She'll have a new family. Her previous circumstances will have nothing to do with her identity because she'll be ours now; she'll be our little baby girl.

In the same way, God wants to give you His nature. When we say "Yes, Lord" to Him, we get to trade the "junk" in our lives for the treasures in His. Romans 8 tells us that we can set aside that spirit of fear and take on a spirit of faith, a spirit of sonship, a conquering spirit, a winning spirit, because when we invite God's Son Jesus into our hearts, we take on His nature, His identity. That means that we can do *all* things through Christ who strengthens us, that we are more than conquerors through Him who loves us. (See Phil. 4;13; Rom. 8:37.)

The Father's Love

If you have never had a dad or experienced a father's love before, Ezekiel 16 tells a story that I believe illustrates how much your heavenly Father loves you. It talks about a prince who was walking along one day, looking out over the fields.[1] As he was walking, he saw something on the ground up ahead that looked as if it were bleeding, and he thought, *Maybe an animal was killed.* Then he saw it move, so he went closer.

To his great surprise he found a newborn baby girl. She was flailing around and kicking; there was life left in her, but there was also blood everywhere. This precious little baby had just been born and had been left there to die, yet she had the will to live; she was holding on to life.

He bent down and picked her up, and as he held her in his arms, he said to her, "I don't care where you're from, I don't care about the circumstances, I don't care who left you here to die. When others say die, I say live."

In this present generation, there is death screaming at you from every different angle—whether it's MTV, music, movies, books, magazines, television, or the Internet, death and hopelessness are all over. God offers us life; He says to us, "Live!" Society's perception of the truth warps the mind and cloaks the eyes from the true hunger of the heart—to be loved and accepted and live the kind of life that brings freedom, happiness, and true contentment. That comes from being empowered with God's Word and walking daily in His Presence.

You may feel as though you don't have any kick left in you, as though you want to stop and give up. I want you to know that God sees you right where you are, just as the prince saw that helpless baby lying on the ground. God wants to pick you up and let you experience His love. He wants you to know that He is ready to move in your life and turn the tide from destruction to restoration:

> I made you grow like a plant of the field. You grew up and developed and became the most beautiful of jewels.
>
> Ezekiel 16:7

It is my great desire that this devotional will encourage and help you to seek God with a new determination and to develop an intimate relationship with Him. When you do, He can help you to commit to a lifestyle of purity, devotion, and courage, and fulfill the plans He has designed just for you—and you will have the time of your life doing it! As you read each entry, open your heart to Him, and allow Him to reveal Himself to you as the faithful, loving Father He is.

The Journey

Seeing the Sights

Part 1

by Susanna Aughtman

Adventuring with God—it is something that is different for each
soul. No snowflake follows the same path from heaven, and no
person walks the same road with God. Our journey is as unique as
our thumbprints, which makes for some uncharted territory. This
allows for some amazing dilemmas and unexpected joy, daily
benefits, and overwhelming mercies along the way.

By the time I reached the correct gate in JFK International Airport
after running for my connecting flight, I was sweating profusely and
had left my new hat and gloves behind in the mad dash. I had a
feeling of sweet relief as I saw my sister Jenny and her friend
Kristin approaching me. The dream of a lifetime was about to be
realized: We were Paris bound.

We squeezed ourselves into our middle coach seats, a bad
selection for any overseas flight, and popped some over-the-
counter medicine to aid us in sleeping through the flight. We
wanted to arrive in Paris wide-eyed and refreshed, but the medicine didn't do its job. Needless to say, we were red-eyed and achy
all over when we arrived at 9 A.M. Paris time. We may have felt a
little dazed and had morning breath, but we were excited because
we were about to experience Paris in all of its splendor.

Paris—a New Name

As we waited for our luggage, my sister Jenny turned and looked at Kristin and me and said, "Let's pick new European-sounding names to go by while we are here. I'll be Genevieve." Kristin was up for it so she decided on Charlemagne. I was trying to decide what name to stick myself with for the next five days...Lorraine? Paulette? Marie? And then it came to me—Brigitte. Lovely Brigitte Bardot, the legendary French actress whose acting career spanned the late 1950s to early 1970s, was glamorous, elegant, metropolitan, and exotic.

I looked nothing like Brigitte Bardot. I had been wearing the same underwear for two days, my eyes were bloodshot, and I felt like if I could find a bed I could sleep my entire vacation away. Tucked away somewhere in my sleep-deprived mind was the desire to be all that I was not. With the magic and allure of this city, I thought I could pull off being a Brigitte. Brigitte was the name that held the aspiration of all that I hoped to be.

Two thousand years ago, something similar happened to a man named Simon. He was coarse and rough. He wasn't a priest or a scholar. He was a Jewish fisherman in a country oppressed by the Roman government. He had leadership qualities mixed with the reality of fear. I'm not sure what his aspirations were, but they probably didn't extend too far past the hope of catching tomorrow's breakfast, let alone catching a glimpse of the Messiah.

As Jesus told him to "follow me" (Matt. 4:18), what Simon didn't realize was that he was about to begin his journey, a journey that would turn his world upside down and his heart inside out. And it all began with a name change.

Read John 1:35-42. Write out verse 42.

Jesus took one look at Simon and saw a name change was in order. His name was *Simon,* but that name didn't hold all that he could hope to be. It told the story of who he was but not who he would become as he journeyed with Jesus. He was going to be a rock—strong, immovable, withstanding great amounts of pressure, someone you could count on. With his name change, Peter received Christ's affirmation. It was if Jesus was saying, "I see who you are, but now I am telling you who you are going to be with Me walking next to you." Every time Jesus called Peter by name, He affirmed him one more time. I wonder how many times Jesus said Peter's name each day. When Jesus tells you every day that you are going to be a rock, strong and mighty, you tend to believe it.

How do you see yourself; what is your "name"? Is it weakness? fear? hurt? anger? unworthy? mediocrity? friendless? Is it strength? courage? peace? worthy? extraordinary? friend?

Write your description below.

5

How does Jesus want to change your name? How do you think that He sees you? If you're having trouble getting started, here are a few ideas: beloved, child of God, chosen one, one-of-a-kind creation, companion—you get the picture.

List your new names, the names that you are and will become as you journey with Christ.

The new names God wants to give you recognize who you are now and describe your eternal potential. When you journey with God, He turns your world upside down and your heart inside out. (See Ezek. 36:26.)

Versailles—a Daily Benefit

Jenny and I embarked on a day trip to Versailles, which involved a forty-minute train ride out of Paris. We got off the train a little dismayed that it didn't drop us off right in front of the Palace of Versailles, home of the famed Marie Antoinette. A businessman happened to be passing by, and I decided to ask him in halting French if he knew the way. He kindly proceeded to tell me in French how to get there.

Our confusion must have been apparent, because to our great delight, he took us by the hand, led us up the street around several bends, and brought us into full view of the most incredible palace we had ever seen. We spent the next three hours viewing amazing opulence and style, perfect gardens, and royal décor. We even got to see where Marie Antoinette had kept a small farm so she could pretend she was living back at home in Austria. All we had to do was ask.

On the way back to the train station, we didn't ask for directions—mistake number one—and we were hopelessly lost for two hours. We succeeded in missing our train and had to wait for the next one, so by the time we arrived back in Paris, it was so late that we missed meeting Kristin. The point is, it's important to ask.

Jesus lets us know in His Word that this works for Him, too. Ask Him for what you need—direction, peace, joy, friendship, blessings—and the benefits will follow.

Read Matthew 7:7-11. Write out verse 7.

This is a great verse to read to yourself each morning when you get out of bed. Do you actually converse with God about your needs? In His perfect timing, He will supply them all according to His riches in glory. (See Phil. 4:19.)

Reflections

List three needs that God has supplied this last year.

_____

_____

_____

List the three greatest needs that you are feeling at this time, whether they are physical, spiritual, emotional, financial, or social.

_____

_____

_____

7

Jesus cares about all of these areas of your life, and He desires to see your needs met. Remember, as Matthew 7:11 says: "If you, then, though you are evil, know how to give good gifts to your children, how much more will your Father in heaven give good gifts to those who ask Him!"

Write today's date next to your need. When your prayers have been answered, be sure to write that date next to the need, too. Your Companion on this journey has the ability to bridge every gap, feed every hunger, and soothe your very soul. He is your Daily Benefit.

Seeing the Sights

Part 2

by Susanna Aughtman

Le Mont-Saint-Michel— a Divine Revelation

Le Mont-Saint-Michel is an abbey that was built hundreds of years ago on a tiny island off of the coast of Northern France. At night, it looks like a fairy castle lit up with lights. We had arrived late one evening to find that the island had shut down and that the only thing left to do was to go to bed. We had a pitiful dinner of dry cereal and settled in for the night.

Jenny and I were sleeping in a double bed with a severe dent in the middle and resigned ourselves to a night of discomfort.

We were almost asleep when Kristin realized she needed to use the restroom. She asked me to turn on the light. I reached up to a small wall lamp above me, feeling for the switch. I did not find the switch. Instead, I happened upon the filaments of a broken light bulb, which sent a surge of 220 volts of electricity coursing through my body. I let out a scream, something akin to the sound of a dying she-bear, and was catapulted onto the body of my hysterical sister.

Surely there has never been as much laughter experienced on the island of Le Mont-Saint-Michel! I don't think I will ever feel as alive as I did the moment I became a human light bulb; my body tingled for minutes afterwards.

Coming into contact with the Creator of the world is equally electrifying.

Do you remember how you felt when you realized how much God loves you? Can you describe your feelings? I felt amazed that God would love me, when I am such a sinner

You don't often comprehend the magnitude of what is happening to you as a child of God until you know the Source that you are drawing from.

List the following names of God.

Revelation 1:8 Alpha, Omega, Almighty

Psalm 144:2 fortress, stronghold, deliver

John 15:1 True vine

John 6:35 bread of Life

John 14:6 way truth Life

John 1:29 Lamb of God

These are only a few of His names. Locate five more names in the Bible on your own.

Son, Messiah

Revel in the new understanding of who God is and the fact that He is the traveling Companion for your journey. When He shows Himself to you, you will never be the same. He awakens your sleeping soul, and this awakening will leave you tingling for all of eternity.

Home to San Francisco— the Journey Continues

Seeing the sights in Paris is an experience I will never forget. Every time you experience something new and exciting, it not only shapes how you see the world, but how you see yourself. There are many wonders that God holds for you on your journey, this path that you walk with others that is uniquely your own. No one else will see all that you see or feel all that you feel or touch all that you touch. That is why God created you and redeemed you and made you His own.

God loves you with a wonderful, unconditional love, and He cannot wait to continue the journey with you. This will be the ultimate journey of your life! It will take you straight to the Father heart of God and eventually bring you to see Him face to glorious face.

Reflections

Tell how the revelation of God's love continues to work in your life as you walk with Him every day.

The Road
Less Traveled

by Vicky Olsen

Traveling on a journey involves deciding which roads to take. The same is true for your life. Jesus said that the road that leads to destruction is broad, but the road that leads to life is narrow. (See Matt. 7:13,14.) Here are two different roads in life that you could take right now. Which one is familiar to you?

Broad Road	Narrow Road
Unsaved friends	Christian friends
Unsaved boyfriend	Christian boyfriend
Drugs, alcohol, smoking	Drug-, alcohol-, and nicotine-free
Secular music	Christian music
Quitting school	Earning your high school diploma
Disobeying parents	Honoring parents with your actions
Not involved in church or church youth group	Active in church and youth group
Foul language	Wholesome language
No regular devotional life	Daily devotional life

R-rated movies and questionable TV	Clean entertainment
Rebellious attitude	Christlike attitude

The broad road is the road that many young people are taking. Peer pressure, low self-esteem, and a difficult home life are among the deciding factors of this choice. It is definitely the easier road to take, and by far, it is the most popular. But in the long run, this road will lead to the destruction of your mind, your body, and your spiritual well-being.

God doesn't give us rules to follow because He is mean or wants to spoil all our "fun." He loves us, He knows what is best for us, and He wants only the best for us. He also knows what will destroy us, and He seeks to keep us from needlessly ruining our lives by showing us in His Word how we are to live.

Let's take a look at what God says about some familiar "roads" in our life.

Friends/Boyfriend

Do not be yoked together with unbelievers. For what do righteousness and wickedness have in common? Or what fellowship can light have with darkness?…What does a believer have in common with an unbeliever?

2 Corinthians 6:14,15

This verse does not mean that Christians should never associate with non-Christians. But it is best if your close relationships are limited to Christian friends because their standards will be the same as yours. Unbelieving friends will not understand why you do or don't do certain things, and they will most likely pressure you to go against your beliefs. *Never* date a non-Christian, thinking that you will "save" him. Before you know it, you may fall in love with him and feel that you cannot leave him.

The next time you are in church, take a look around. How many wives do you see sitting without their husbands? If you ask them, many would probably tell you that they dated men they believed would someday get saved, but they never did. That is not God's best, so don't let that happen to you. Only date someone who loves the Lord as much as you do, and serve Him together.

Drugs/Alcohol/Smoking

Do not get drunk on wine, which leads to debauchery. Instead, be filled with the Spirit.

Ephesians 5:18

Do you not know that your body is a temple of the Holy Spirit, who is in you, whom you have received from God? You are not your own;

you were bought at a price. Therefore honor God with your body.

1 Corinthians 6:19,20

Drugs, alcohol, and cigarette smoking all destroy the body, and the body should be valued by the Christian as a sacred place where God dwells (when we invite His Son Jesus into our hearts). These physical addictions can lead to psychological and spiritual damage, and the use of any of these substances ruins our Christian witness.

Music/Movies/TV/Computer

… whatever is true, whatever is noble, whatever is right, whatever is pure, whatever is lovely, whatever is admirable—if anything is excellent or praiseworthy—think about such things.

Philippians 4:8

What we listen to with our ears and watch with our eyes is what will occupy our thoughts and our minds. And what occupies our minds is what influences our speech and our actions. As a believer

13

it should be impossible to watch anything that blasphemes God by their profanity and indecent subject matter. If you are not sure that a particular movie, program, or Web site is suitable to watch, ask yourself this question: *What would Jesus do? Would He watch it? Would He listen to it?*

School

> The plans of the diligent lead to profit as surely as haste leads to poverty.
>
> Proverbs 21:5

Do not take a shortcut when your future is at stake. Many teens quit school to work full time, because they think that making money is more important than finishing high school. But patience and planning for the future by earning a high school diploma can only benefit you.

Although college is not for everyone, it would be well worth your time to at least consider the possibility of furthering your education by exploring all options, whether it be higher education at a university, Bible college, or community college, or some type of vocational training.

Parents

> …obey your parents in the Lord, for this is right.
> "Honor your father and mother"—which is the first commandment with a promise—
> "that it may go well with you and that you may enjoy long life on the earth."
>
> Ephesians 6:1-3

To honor your parents is more than just to obey them; it is to respect them. This includes listening to their advice and accepting their

14

ground rules, even if you don't always understand them. Colossians 3:20 says that obedience toward parents pleases the Lord. But, remember, that does not mean living in a physically or sexually abusive situation. If that describes you, seek outside help immediately!

Church/Youth Group

> Let us not give up meeting together, as some are in the habit of doing, but let us encourage one another....
>
> Hebrews 10:25

Christians go to church to worship God, to hear the preaching and teaching of the Word, to minister to one another, and to fellowship with other believers. All of these things are necessary for a victorious Christian walk. In addition to attending church regularly, it is important that you be actively involved in a youth group so that you can worship and fellowship with other Christians your age and learn from a youth pastor how to apply God's Word to your individual situation.

15

Language

> Do not let any unwholesome talk come out of your mouths, but only what is helpful for building others up according to their needs, that it may benefit those who listen.
>
> Ephesians 4:29

Unwholesome talk includes obscene and offensive language, participating in gossip, telling (and listening to) crude jokes, and talking bad about other people. The above Scripture tells us that our talk should benefit those who listen to us. Look again at what makes up unwholesome talk. None of these things benefit anyone; instead, they degrade and humiliate you and everyone else involved. And unwholesome talk, in any form, only serves to damage your Christian witness.

Devotional Life

> So I say, live by the Spirit, and you will not gratify the desires of the sinful nature.
>
> Galatians 5:16

Spending time in the Presence of God is the only way we can ensure that our life is controlled by the Holy Spirit. Going to church a couple of times a week is not enough; we must communicate with God on a daily basis. We can do this through prayer and reading His Word.

God desires that we spend quality time alone with Him so that we can grow closer to Him and become more like His Son Jesus Christ. Spending even a few minutes every day praying and reading the Bible is more beneficial than spending a couple of hours once a week with God.

Our minds need to be *continually* renewed by the Holy Spirit if sin is not to have a place in our lives. Make personal devotions a normal part of your daily routine.

Attitude

> … put off your old self, which is being corrupted by its deceitful desires;
>
> to be made new in the attitude of your minds; and to put on the new self, created to be like God in true righteousness and holiness.
>
> Ephesians 4:22-24

An attitude is a state of mind or feeling. Your attitude is your mental outlook on life. God desires that not only our *actions* be Christlike, but our *attitudes* as well. We can be physically forced to conform to Christian standards by our parents, youth pastor, or teachers, but that does not make us Christians. If our attitudes are rebellious, disobedient, defiant, stubborn, or quarrelsome, our

16

hearts are not right with God. A Christlike attitude exhibits those qualities that characterize Christ: righteousness, holiness, meekness, gentleness, kindness, and love.

Do you need an "attitude adjustment"? God will lovingly change your attitude as you spend more time with Him.

Reflections

Have you been "traveling" down the broad road or the narrow road? Why?

_____

_____

_____

_____

17

If your life choices have kept you on the broad road, what can you do to get onto the narrow road?

_____

_____

_____

_____

The Free Gift

Part 1

by Erin E. Zonio

In the movie *The Mission*, the character of Rodrigo Mendoza was in the terrible profession of a slave hunter who plundered the natives in the jungles of South America. These were people who had lived there for centuries, but he was a man with a wicked heart and thought only of himself. On one particular day, after he had sold some natives into slavery, he went to see his brother's wife with whom he was having an affair. His brother walked in on them, and they fought each other in the street. The battle was vicious and ended in bloodshed—Mendoza killed his brother.

Mendoza felt so horrible that he turned himself in to the authorities. He was put in jail, and for several days he meditated on the crime he had committed. He thought of his brother whom he had killed. He realized the selfishness that had led to his brother's death. He then began to reflect on his profession—stealing innocent natives from their homes and selling them to slavery. Overcome by guilt, he refused to eat anything.

Weeks later, a Jesuit priest came to visit him. The priest had been ministering to the very village from which Mendoza had wounded and stolen the natives. He offered Mendoza a chance to make up for the life he had lived so far.

"Come, and make your life count for something," the priest encouraged him.

It took a while to convince Mendoza. He felt like he was worth nothing, that he did not deserve a second chance. Finally, he agreed, but his attitude was that of self-degradation. In order to make penance for his sins, he gathered his swords, armor, and other iron and steel tools used by a slave trader, and tied them in a bundle to his waist so they would drag behind him as he walked. Mendoza and the Jesuit set out for their journey. Under the weight of the baggage, Mendoza strained to take one simple step.

They traveled for several days through the mountainous jungle until they reached the base of a waterfall that began at the top of a cliff hundreds of feet high. The priest looked at Mendoza as if to say, "You don't *have* to haul that baggage around anymore. Why don't you just let it go?" The former slave trader scowled at him and turned toward the waterfall.

The climb beside the waterfall was precarious. Footholds were found only every few feet and were only a few inches deep into the jagged rock. Bare hands and sandaled feet were cut by the sharp stone. The priest and his traveling companions would move up quickly and then look back to find that Mendoza had climbed only one step. A few times, the weight of Mendoza's bundle became too heavy, and he skidded back down the rock.

The priest hurried down after him on one of these occasions and begged, "Let me cut those bundles from you."

Mendoza only growled at him in refusal.

Finally, Mendoza's hands felt the top of the cliff. The priest and the natives who were meeting them at the top pulled Mendoza over the edge, and he collapsed in fatigue. The natives, recognizing him, pulled out their spears and watched him carefully. The leader of the group approached Mendoza, took his spear, and cut the ties to the baggage. The bundle fell over the edge and down into the water hundreds of feet below. Mendoza was free.

Mendoza did not have to pay for his sin and torture himself by hauling those bundles up the waterfall, but he could not accept forgiveness from God. He could not forgive himself. He felt he had to make penance—or *pay*—for his sin.

Many people, like Mendoza, think they can earn God's favor, but salvation by grace is one of the main doctrines that sets Christianity apart from all other religions. Christianity is the only religion that says you do not have to earn a relationship with God to live with Him in heaven forever. We can do nothing that grants us the privilege of being His children. God, through His Son Jesus, has already paid the price. (See 1 Cor. 6:20.) So, in order for us to understand our heavenly Father and to appreciate our salvation, we need to understand grace.

Write out what you believe to be the definition of grace. Why do you think it is important to learn about grace?

20

_____

_____

_____

_____

What Is Grace?

Grace could be described as goodwill, favor, a delay granted for payment of something owed, or the love and favor of God to humankind. Grace implies that something is given to or done for someone without expecting anything in return.

Let's say, for example, your friend gives you a nice new pair of earrings just because she thought of you when she saw them. You immediately like them, and as you are modeling them for her, she says, "By the way, they cost me ten dollars." If you pay her back for the earrings, you essentially bought them yourself. On the other hand, if she gave you the earrings and did not expect you to pay her, they were truly a gift.

A Biblical Definition

The first time I can remember grace being defined for me was when I was in junior high. Our Sunday school teacher taught us this acronym:

God's

Riches

At

Christ's

Expense

What does this acronym mean to you? _____

_____

_____

This definition lays an excellent foundation for us to understand the grace of God. Christ bought a gift for me; therefore, I can enjoy all the blessings of knowing God.

I used to think God saved me because I was special. I thought I was a Christian because I did the right thing. I soon became tired of feeling like I had to be born again every time I made a wrong choice. I was weary from trying to earn God's love.

However, through a college course that focused on grace, my relationship with God was changed. I learned that my own right-eousness and my attempts at being good were not what earned my salvation. Christ gave me the opportunity to be a Christian *while I was still a sinner*. I did not earn my salvation; my salvation is a gift from God that He bought for me with the shed blood of Jesus Christ. (See 1 Pet. 1:18,19.)

Read Romans 5:6-8. Which phrase in this passage means the most to you? _____

_____

We can come to God just as we are. One of the great old hymns describes it this way: "Just as I am, without one plea, but that Thy blood was shed for me, and that Thou biddest me come to Thee...."[1] This tells us that we can come to the Lord because He paid the price for our sins, we can enter into His Presence because He longs for us to do so, and we can enjoy His blessings because He loves us. It is only by His grace.

Reflections

Read John 1:12. How does one become a Christian?

If this is all that it takes to become a Christian, who does all the work?

Think about what you were like before you were a Christian. What earned you the right to be born again?

If you answered "nothing," then you understand that God has saved you by His grace. You understand that you didn't do anything to deserve God's grace. You just heard His Spirit speaking to your heart, and you said, "Yes, Lord, I'll take it."

Our salvation is free to us!

22

The Free Gift

Part 2

The Law of God and the Grace of God

by Erin E. Zonio

Centuries before Christ came to earth to purchase salvation for us, God gave His people the Ten Commandments. (See Ex. 20:1-17.) These rules were to be strictly followed, and when they were broken, there were certain conditions they had to meet if they wanted to remain in God's favor. For example, when certain laws were broken, they had to make sacrifices or be cast out of the city to wander in the wilderness or be killed. If God intended all along to save us by grace, why did He ever give us the Law?

Read Romans 7:7-13.

One of the main reasons God gave us the Law is that His Son Jesus had not yet come to earth, shed His blood on the cross, died, and rose again for the sins of humankind. Until then, people's sins had to be atoned according to the Law.

Over the years, though, all these rules became a source of slavery to the people of Israel and the rest of the world. They were constantly faced with their sin, and they were constantly trying to make up for their misdeeds. God had set a high standard in order for the people of Israel to be saved, but no one was able to achieve it. God used the Law to show mankind their need for His grace and mercy.

Read John 1:14. Jesus "came from the Father, full of
_____ *and* _____."

This Scripture tells us that God does not overlook the Law when He graciously grants us the gift of salvation. If that were the case, we would have a compromising and ignorant god. Since He is *full of truth* as the Scripture states, He sees the truth that we are sinners, yet He chooses to give us what we do not deserve.

24

Grace and Mercy

Another way to help us understand God's grace is to compare it to mercy. Throughout the Old Testament, where the Law had to be followed in order to receive salvation, the word "grace" was rarely used. Instead, the word most commonly used to describe God's attitude toward His people was "mercy." There is a difference between the two.

The dictionary defines mercy as "a refraining from harming offenders, enemies, etc."[1] If my mother caught me lying when I was a little girl, she usually washed my mouth out with soap. I deserved it. However, if she caught me and decided not to punish me, that was mercy. Mercy is refraining from giving someone what they deserve. Grace is giving someone what they don't deserve.

People in the Old Testament had a different relationship with God than we do. They felt He was good because He withheld punishment from them.

*Read John 10:10 and finish the sentence: "...but I am
come that they might have life, and that they might have it*

_____.

The New Testament brought the word "grace" into our relationship with God. In addition to viewing God as merciful, now we are
able to enjoy His free, abundant blessing in our lives.

I used to have a 1982 Nissan Sentra—one of the first ever
made! By the time I had attended college in Santa Cruz, California,
my car had many miles on it, and the drive to school was grueling.
In fact, it is known as a very dangerous highway. To protect myself
from getting into an accident, I would play Christian music in the
car as I drove to and from home. I thought that God would
certainly protect me from a collision because I was praising Him
during the drive!

What I did not realize was that I was relying on my own abilities
to earn the blessing of God's protection. This idea goes against the
very concept of grace! God would have protected me whether or
not I played Christian music in the car.

He did not protect me because I deserved it—He protected me
even though *I did not* deserve it! I cannot earn His blessings or His
salvation, and He does not give them to me because I am special.
He pours out His blessings and salvation upon me because He
loves me and because I have simply received His Son Jesus into
my heart and believed on His name.

> In him we have redemption through his blood, the forgiveness of
> sins, in accordance *with the riches of God's grace*
> *that he lavished on us with all wisdom and understanding.*
>
> Ephesians 1:7,8

Reflections

*What does "mercy" mean to you? What does "grace" mean to you?*_____

_____

_____

_____

_____

_____

26

Knowing Your Destination

by Erin E. Zonio

Who's in the Driver's Seat?

Imagine getting in your car on the passenger side. God sits down behind the wheel, and you hand Him the keys. You tell Him, "Okay, God, You're driving. Wherever You want me to go, take me there." God turns on the car, starts driving down the street, then turns left. You think, *Well, I usually turn right here, but He is God, so I'll trust Him. He's the Driver!*

You sit back, and just when you're about to relax and enjoy the drive, He turns left again, and you start heading into an unfamiliar, scary neighborhood. "Uh, God, You *do* know where You're going, don't You?"

"Yes, I'm God. I know everything," He tells you.

As you leave the neighborhood, you find yourself in the middle of nowhere. You're getting a little nervous. Where's God going anyway? "God, I hate to impose, but…would You like me to drive?"

"Don't worry. I've got everything under control."

"Okay," you hesitantly respond. "By the way, where are we headed?"

"Toward the mall."

"Oh! I like the mall!" you exclaim. "It's a good thing we're going there because I want to buy a new outfit."

You relax and turn on the radio. You don't mind which roads God takes because you're headed toward the mall. Besides, He's God, and He knows what He's doing.

Soon the mall is in sight. "I usually park over by the east entrance because the main entrance is really crowded, especially on Saturdays," you suggest.

"I know," God says as He heads toward the west entrance.

"Well, I guess You are God," you admit. "You can park wherever You want." Suddenly, instead of turning left into the parking lot, God turns right, heading away from the mall. "Wait, God! You turned the wrong way—I thought we were going to the mall."

"I never said we were going *to* the mall. I said we were headed *toward* the mall. We were headed toward the mall so we could turn right on this street. I have someplace else I'd like you to go—now is not the time to go to the mall."

One of the more difficult things about living for God is letting Him stay in the driver's seat. We let Him drive for a while, but when we're not confident about where He's taking us, we try to tell Him what to do. We even try to take over. It's also hard when we think we've arrived at our destination, and then He turns in the opposite direction.

Have you allowed God to be in the driver's seat of your life?

Read Jeremiah 29:11 and fill in the blanks:

"For I know the plans I have for you," declares the Lord. "Plans to _____ you and not to harm you, plans to give you _____ and a _____."

God knows where you are headed; He has a plan. Sometimes we think that His plan might be boring or unsatisfying, but the following verses show just the opposite:

Write out John 10:10. _____

_____

_____

Write out Psalm 34:7. _____

_____

We should trust God even when we are unsure of where He's taking us. By allowing Him to remain in the driver's seat of your life, you're allowing Him to lead you to a life of satisfaction and abundance.

Which Path Will You Take?

In this journey of life, there are many decisions we must make; some are small, and others are significant. These choices include what college we will attend and what we will study, whom we will marry, where we will live, and more. God wants to lead you to the right decisions, because these choices influence what your final destination will be.

There are some people to whom God speaks very clearly and directly regarding the decisions they have to make. For most people, though, God speaks through our circumstances, through the quiet voice we hear in our hearts, through His Word that we read, or even through other people. If you want to know God's will for your life, ask Him to guide you, and then consider these five factors as you make your decisions:

God's Gifts • What talents has God given me? What circumstances are influencing my decision?

God's Word • What decision would be consistent with God's character and will?

God's People • What have other believers said to me regarding my future? How have others encouraged me?

God's Voice • What do I sense the Holy Spirit speaking to my heart?

God's Plan • Will this help me in my pursuit of the final destination, to be like Jesus?

When these five factors seem to point you in a certain direction that is consistent with the Bible, you can be confident that He is leading you in that path.

Your Final Destination

Recently, my family and I flew to California to visit relatives. The airline attendant asked each person who approached the counter, "What is your final destination?" There were many different answers. Some people were going to Santa Barbara, others were going to Cincinnati, and others were headed out of the country. It was important for the travelers to know their final destination so they could be certain they'd get there.

In order for us to get somewhere, we need to know where we're going. The problem is that few people, including Christians, know what their ultimate destination in life is.

As Christians, what do you think is our final destination?

_____

_____

_____

God's plan for each and every Christian is found in Romans 8:29. Write it out here: _____

_____

_____

In your own words, for what has God predestined all of us?

_____

_____

Part of God's plan for us is to become like His Son Jesus. In order to become Christlike, we need to get to know Him. We can do this through our personal experiences with Him and also through reading and studying the Bible.

Read the following Scriptures and identify the qualities Jesus is displaying in each of these scenarios. Use the word bank below to help you get started, and add any other qualities you can think of. (There can be more than one for each Scripture):

Matthew 15:29-32 _____

Luke 4:1-12 _____

Luke 15:4-6 _____

John 3:14-16 _____

John 8:1-11 _____

John 10:14,15 _____

John 13:3-10 _____

Forgiving	Gentle
Compassionate	Holy
Faithful	Kind
Loving	Servant

Psalm 139:16 says, "…All the days ordained for me were written in your [God's] book before one of them came to be." Before you were even conceived, God had a purpose for *your* life that could not be fulfilled by any other person. Sometimes we think that God's call is always to a specific place for the rest of our life. Usually, however, His call is to a specific place for a certain amount of time. God uses your present circumstances to prepare you for the next situation, and that situation will prepare you for the following one. He uses the uphill times and the downhill times, the U-turns, and the curves in the road to prepare you for your ultimate destination.

Throughout junior high and high school, I wanted nothing more for my future than to fulfill God's call on my life. While this showed sincere devotion to God, I also had a misunderstanding about the will of God. I told our youth pastor, "I'm just so afraid that I'm going to miss out on God's will for my life."

God's will is not so mysterious and out-of-reach that unless you walk a perfectly fine line, you will miss it. His biggest desire is that you walk with Him and seek Him.

Deuteronomy 10:12-13 says, "And now, O Israel, what does the Lord your God ask of you but to fear the Lord your God, to walk in all his ways, to love him, to serve the Lord your God with all your heart and with all your soul, and to observe the Lord's commands and decrees…?" As you do this, He will lead you into His good, perfect, and satisfying will for your life, and He will lead you to your destination.

32

Reflections

Based on the decisions you are making now, what will your final destination be? _____

_____

_____

Are the decisions you have been making leading you in that direction? Why or why not? _____

_____

_____

If not, what can you do to make a U-turn and start heading in the right direction? _____

_____

Finding True Love

by Shereen Christian

Do you have a picture in your mind of the perfect wedding? Most of us start daydreaming about our wedding day when we are little girls. Mine went something like this.

I would arrive at the church in a white and gold horse-drawn carriage wearing a beautiful princess-for-a-day dress. The dress would have a 10-foot train that was encrusted with tiny crystal beads. Every time the light caught them just right, they would shimmer brilliantly, just as if they were hundreds of little white diamonds.

White roses arranged in gold vases four feet high would be placed beside every row of seats along the aisle. There would be tapered candles in candelabras casting a soft, golden light throughout the church. My bridesmaids would all be dressed in beautiful floor-length gowns, each one carrying a single white rose surrounded in baby's breath and tied together with a silk bow. Flower girls wearing satin and lace dresses and carrying delicate baskets would scatter soft pink rose petals all over the floor.

Up at the altar, dressed in a black tuxedo with one white rose bud pinned to his lapel, would be the man of my dreams—the one who would love me forever, cherish, honor, and protect me from harm. He would provide for me, encourage me, and accept me just as I am. He would be my "best friend," be there when I need him, uplift me, and defend me. He would even die for me. My "prince charming."

> Long ago the Lord said to Israel: "I have loved you, my people, with an everlasting love. With unfailing love I have drawn you to myself."
>
> Jeremiah 31:3 NLT

Whether you want your fairy tale wedding to be a lot like mine or completely different, one thing remains the same: We all want "prince charming" waiting for us at the altar. We all want someone on whose love we can depend, and who accepts us unconditionally. If we don't know the awesome love of Jesus, all we are left with is whatever illusion the world has to offer.

The following is my story.

I wanted my "prince charming" to be more than just a husband. I wanted him to be my "savior." He would be the one to rescue me from a life that, at times, hardly seemed worth living.

Things that were happening at home were pretty tough for me growing up. To the outside world I'm sure my life looked great, but behind closed doors it was quite a different story, one of violence and abuse. There were times when the screaming and yelling, the horrible, cruel words, and the fighting were more than I could bear. Then there were other times when the cold, awkward silence seemed deafening.

Unfortunately, praise, support, and encouragement were not a part of my young world. My parents were so unhappy with each other that all those negative emotions just kind of spilled over onto the kids. There were not many loving looks, gentle touches, or kind words spoken to me or about me. In fact, every memory I have of an adult speaking my name as a child is with a harsh or impatient tone in their voice.

I grew up feeling very guilty and ashamed of myself. I was left feeling that no matter what I did it would never be good enough. I would never be good enough. So, I spent most of my time believing that "if only" I were prettier, sweeter, smarter, funnier, I would be happy; I would be loved.

When I was in high school, I decided to change all that. I tried anything and almost everything to earn other people's approval and love. I tried to be prettier, sweeter, smarter, and funnier, hang out with the right people, wear the right clothes, you name it—I did it. Oh, sure, for a while all my efforts actually worked—or so I thought.

I was popular, dated lots of guys, and since I didn't see love modeled in my home nor did I know how loved and valued I was by God, I pretty much thought that all this attention was equal to love. And I was going to hold on to it no matter what the cost. I didn't see the temptation as a trap and walked right into the snare.

Every time I turned around, it seemed like the stakes were getting higher and higher. Soon, being pretty wasn't enough. Girls were expected to be sexy. Dressing "in-style" became more and more provocative and revealing. Before I knew what was happening, I was so caught up in trying to be what everyone around me wanted me to be that I completely lost myself in the process. As I said earlier, for a while, I was able to pull it off, but in the end, I was left with a life that was spiraling out of control.

As I got older, my "if-only's" changed a bit—"If only" I met the right guy, had the right career, drove the right car. But one thing remained the same—I was still willing to do just about anything to earn people's approval and love. The sad thing was that I was convinced nobody could love me if they knew the "real" me. So I just continued on with this charade, being this person I knew I wasn't but too lost to remember who I was.

By now my life looked a lot like the home I grew up in. Great on the outside—I had a handsome husband, a beautiful home, and a great career—but on the inside, I was filled with emptiness, loneliness, and pain. All those years of trying to fill the void, all the choices I made, they all seemed to add up to nothing. And even though to the world it looked like I had it all, I had a sinking feeling in my heart that this counterfeit existence was all there was.

Then one Sunday morning something happened that changed my life forever. I met a Prince—the One who would love me

35

forever, cherish, honor, and protect me from harm, provide for me, encourage me, and accept me just as I am. He would be my Best Friend, be there when I need Him, uplift me, and defend me. He even died for me.

Suddenly, there it was—the love and acceptance I had been searching for my whole life! In an instant I was changed. The unworthiness I felt inside was gone. The longing was replaced with belonging. And all the pain, confusion, and rejection were wiped away by one touch of His hand. He was there all along, waiting for me to say yes, waiting for me to invite Him into my heart and into my life, waiting for me to accept Him as my Prince, my Lord, my Savior. I met Jesus, and I became a princess in the greatest love story of all.

Reflections

Have you ever done or said anything just to win the approval of others? If so, how did it make you feel afterwards?

_____

_____

_____

Have you ever found yourself doing something that you never thought you would? _____

_____

_____

How would you describe yourself? _____

_____

_____

_____

What do you think your friends and/or family would say to describe you? _____

_____

_____

How does God describe you? What does His Word say about you? Look up the following three Scriptures. Next to each Scripture describe yourself based on who God says you are.

Deuteronomy 7:6 _____

_____

_____

Colossians 3:12 _____

_____

37

_____

1 John 3:1 _____

_____

_____

God loves you so much. He loves you with an unfailing love. He has chosen you and called you by name. You are a special treasure to Him.

Is Jesus waiting for you? Have you invited Him into your heart? If not and you would like to, remember, there's a prayer you can pray at the end of this book.

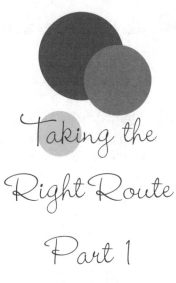

Taking the

Right Route

Part 1

by Tanya DeVoll

Imagine yourself lost on a country road. You've wandered away from the others, and you are trying to find your way home. You come to a fork in the road, and you don't know which way to turn. You have a choice to make, and you are starting to get worried as night is falling. How are you going to know which way to go? How are you ever going to get home? Nothing looks familiar, and you have no idea what to do. A wrong turn and you could be lost in the woods with wild animals. You fall to your knees and cry out to your heavenly Father.

We have all been at this kind of place in our lives where we've been lost, and we don't know which way to turn.

Write down a brief description of a time when you were lost, how you felt while you were lost, and how you were found.

_____

_____

_____

_____

_____

On your journey of life, God wants to lead you and guide you in the little questions as well as the big ones. He wants to help you in moral dilemmas and with questions, such as *What am I going to do with my life?* and *How will I get to where God wants me to go?* As you read on, I hope to help you answer some of those uncertainties.

God's Route for Your Life

Before discussing how to take the right route, first you need to focus on the route itself. Your life journey has already been planned out by God. Did you know that He designed you just the way you are on purpose? He has big plans for you and made you just as you are so He can do special things with your life.

39

Write out Jeremiah 29:11-13.

_____

_____

_____

From this passage you can see that God does have a plan for your life, and He wants you to know that to give you hope for the future. It goes on to tell you that if you seek God with all your heart, you will find Him and discover those plans. Do you have a deep desire to do what is right and to make the right choices in life? God has given you the Bible as one of the best ways to stay on track.

Read Psalm 1:1-3 and put it in your own words.

_____

_____

_____

_____

Three Ways To Stay on the Right Route

As a young person, you have your whole life in front of you. Maybe you have already made some poor choices, but God promises us in Isaiah 43:25, "I, even I, am he who blots out your transgressions, for My own sake, and remembers your sins no more." You can begin to ask God to help you make right choices and to seek Him for the big decisions you have to make. (See Prov. 15:29; 1 John 5:14,15.) When you come to the end of your life, won't it be wonderful to have Jesus look in your face and say, "Well done, good and faithful servant!" as He did to the man in Matthew 25 who used his talents to the fullest? (See v. 21.)

In my life there have been three things that I have used to stay on track and to help me make right choices—Bible reading, prayer, and accountability. Because they are an important part of every believer's life, we're going to take a look at them individually.

Before we do, describe your involvement in each of these areas in your life right now:

Bible Reading _____

_____

_____

_____

Prayer _____

_____

_____

_____

40

Accountability _____

_____

_____

1. The Road of Bible Reading

My life was transformed when I graduated from high school. I had been a Christian all my life, but I entered an intense discipleship program to take my relationship with God to a higher level. It was in beautiful southern California that I discovered the discipline of reading the Bible every day. I bought a prayer journal that guided me in reading the Bible through in a year, and my life has never been the same.

I used to sit every day and read on a cliff that overlooked a deserted canyon. I could see for miles in the natural, but I could also see my future brighten as I filled my life with God's promises. As I opened my heart, God would speak to me about changes I needed to make. Every day there was something in His Word that really touched me, and I would write those verses down.

41

Once the year was up and I had read through the entire Bible for the first time, I looked back and saw how God was using those Scriptures to keep me headed in the right direction.

Second Timothy 3:16-17 tell us, "All Scripture is God-breathed and is useful for teaching, rebuking, correcting and training in righteousness, so that the man of God may be thoroughly equipped for every good work." Not only does Scripture tell us how valuable it is for our lives, but millions of people all around the world have put the Word to practice and have seen how God has used it to help guide them and keep them doing the right things.

The Bible is one of the ingredients to make your life pleasing to the Lord. He has given you His Word to help guide your life.

Reflections

Here are some verses that describe the Word. Match each verse with what you think it is teaching us:

Verses

1. Psalm 119:9 _____

2. Psalm 119:11 _____

3. Psalm 119:105 _____

4. Hebrews 4:12 _____

5. James 1:22 _____

42

Teach us

A. We will be blessed if we do what the Bible says.

B. The Word can keep our ways pure.

C. The Bible guides us.

D. The Word judges our attitudes and thoughts.

E. Scriptures memorized help us to not sin.

If you want to stay on the right path to where God wants you to go, then read His Word daily, and it will guide you and help keep you pure.

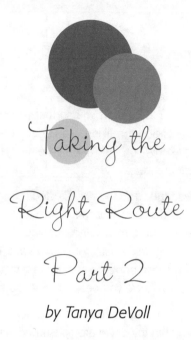

Taking the

Right Route

Part 2

by Tanya DeVoll

Let's continue looking at things we can use to stay on track in our walk with God.

2. The Path of Prayer

First Thessalonians 5:17 tells us to "pray continually." What other instructions do you need? Prayer is the key to unlocking intimacy with God, and it is where God can change you. It is in the secret, quiet place that you will begin to feel the heartbeat of God for a lost and dying world. It is where you will begin to know Him and know His plans for your life.

Let's look at some verses that will show us how prayer will help keep you on the right route:

Write out Philippians 4:6. _____

_____

This verse is used to comfort you so that you do not worry about your future or about making wrong decisions. God will give you the peace to know you are making the right decisions when you seek Him for answers.

Peace has been the way God has directed me the most. I have had to make many decisions, such as where to go to college, what to do after college, who to marry, and what jobs to take. I have hardly seen the "handwriting on the wall" or seen visions. Mostly I have had this overwhelming sense of peace after praying that I was following the right path. God will give you peace, too, if you seek Him.

When we decide to do what we know is right, we have peace. When we do our own thing, we are consumed with guilt. God is at work in us in those times to keep us on the right track.

Write out Mark 11:24-25. _____

_____

What does this verse mean to you? _____

_____

_____

Write out Matthew 6:33. _____

_____

_____

44

God wants you to put Him first in your life, and then everything else will fall into place. Seek Him first, and He promises you that you will be charting out the correct course for your life.

3. The Passage of Accountability

Accountability is another way to help you get to where God wants you to go. You need to keep in contact with your friends to maintain a friendship with them, but some people forget that you need to do the same thing with your Savior.

Church attendance is one kind of accountability.

What church do you attend now? _____

How many times a week do you attend? _____

Do you attend youth group? _____

Do you attend Sunday school? _____

Do you attend Sunday morning worship? _____

Hebrews 10:25 says, "Let us not give up meeting together, as some are in the habit of doing, but let us encourage one another— and all the more as you see the Day approaching."

Church is a place where you can get help to keep you on the right track. In a church where people care about you, there is accountability. Has someone ever asked you why you weren't at church lately, or have you asked that of someone else? God wants us to encourage each other to be dedicated to Him with our whole hearts. Verse 24 says, "Let us consider how we may spur one another on toward love and good deeds." God will use other Christians in your life not only to lift you up and encourage you in your faith walk, but to urge you to love God with all your heart.

A second type of accountability is personal accountability.

Another way that you can keep on the right track and follow God's will for your life is to find someone you can trust to keep you accountable. Find someone you can meet with on a weekly or biweekly basis, someone you can pour out your heart to, someone who is a good listener. It would be best if this person were a little older than you, but the important thing is to find someone you can be honest with, someone who will not be afraid of asking you hard questions, such as, "Have you been praying and reading your Bible?" Or, "Are you involved in anything that you know you should not be?"

If you do not already have a friend like this, pray and ask God to send someone your way. You could even ask your youth pastor's wife or pastor's wife to help keep you accountable. Maybe someone else in your youth group really needs a friend, and you can keep her accountable.

46

Reflections

Name a friend whom you would like to begin an accountability relationship with. _____

God has provided you with three compasses to keep you on the right route for your journey in life—Bible reading, prayer, and accountability. You will never be lost with these guiding your life.

"Where Have You Come From, Where Are You Going?"

by Vicky Olsen

A young girl, tears streaming down her face, frantically gathers what few belongings she has as she plots her plan of escape. "I can't take it anymore," she whispers to herself. "I must go away; I must go where they can't find me." In a frenzied state, she grabs her knapsack and heads out into the darkness.

Who is this young girl? Could it possibly be you, or somebody you know? Would it surprise you to know that she lived almost 4000 years ago? The girl's name was Hagar. Hagar was probably about your age, and as we will see next, she experienced struggles and difficulties as many young people do. Hagar did not know where she was going in life—do you?

Read Genesis 16:7-8: "The angel of the Lord found Hagar near a spring in the desert; it was the spring that is beside the road to Shur. And he said, 'Hagar, servant of Sarai [Sarah], where have you come from, and where are you going?'"

"I'm running away from my mistress, Sarah," she answered. Who was Hagar, and why was she running away?

Hagar was the Egyptian maid of Sarah, Abraham's wife. Abraham and Sarah had lived in Egypt for a while because of a famine in the land of Canaan. They probably acquired Hagar while they were living there.

At that time Sarah could not have any children. Even though God had promised Abraham that he would be a father, Sarah grew impatient and gave him Hagar to be his wife and bear children for them. Because Hagar was Sarah's servant, she had no choice but to obey Sarah and do whatever she was told to do. Although this may sound very strange to us, it was actually "socially acceptable" in the Near East during that time.

However, Sarah sinned by giving Hagar to Abraham to be his wife because Sarah tried to obtain God's blessing through her own effort. Sarah's actions caused heartache and grief for herself, for Abraham, and especially for Hagar. As a result, the relationship between Sarah and Hagar grew tense.

What are some examples of things that are "socially acceptable" today but are displeasing to God?

48

_____

_____

_____

Have you ever run away from home or felt like running away from home? Why?

_____

_____

_____

Maybe you have been hurt or disappointed by a family member or a friend. Perhaps you trusted someone who let you down. Any of these situations in our lives can cause us to become angry and bitter toward people who have hurt us. The problem is that anger and bitterness can turn into hatred over a period of time. But God has given us a miracle that can erase the hurt, the bitterness, the anger, and the hatred we feel. The miracle is called *forgiveness,* an issue that we will look at more later on.

When Hagar became pregnant, the Bible tells us that she began to look down on Sarah, so Sarah mistreated her. As Sarah's personal maid, Hagar enjoyed special privileges that the other servant girls did not have. To punish Hagar, Sarah probably made her sleep where the rest of the servant girls slept, and most likely forced her to do the filthy and messy jobs that were usually performed by the other servants. How humiliating that must have been for Hagar! That is why she ran away. (See Gen. 16:6.)

In Genesis 16:8 the angel of the Lord asked Hagar two very important questions: where she had come from and where she was going. Hagar said that she was running away from her mistress, Sarah. Notice she answered the angel's first question but not the angel's second question.

Why didn't Hagar tell the angel where she was going?

It is very possible that she did not know where she was going.

Verse 7 tells us that the angel found Hagar near a spring in the desert beside the road to Shur, a city that is located close to the border of Egypt. It would seem that Hagar was returning to Egypt! She was probably ashamed to tell the angel that she was leaving the place where she had first heard about the Lord and that she was going back to a land that worshipped idols.

Hagar's running away from her mistress, Sarah, and returning to Egypt can be compared to our running away from God when we are discouraged and retreating back into the world. Often God uses something in the Old Testament (a person, a nation, or an object) to represent something else in the New Testament. This is called *typology.* The nation of Egypt is sometimes used to symbolize the world in the New Testament. In the Old Testament, the Israelites were slaves in the land of Egypt. Today, we are slaves to sin and worldly things before we ask Jesus Christ to come into our hearts.

What was your life like before you became a Christian? If you are not a Christian, what is your life like now?

_____

_____

_____

The Bible tells us that while the Israelites wandered in the desert after Moses had led them out of Egypt, they grumbled because they longed for the food and meat they had eaten while slaves in Egypt. The Israelites only remembered the good things in Egypt. (See Gen. 16:3.) That's what happens when people backslide. They only remember the "fun" of sin; they forget all the heartache and guilt that go along with it.

What are some of the things you are pressured to do by class-mates, unsaved friends, or family members that you know a Christian should not do? What are their consequences?

_____

_____

_____

Look at verse 9 of Genesis 16.

What did the angel of the Lord tell Hagar to do?

_____

_____

Because Hagar was obedient to the Lord and did as the angel instructed her to do, God blessed her by making her the mother of an entire nation. If we are faithful to God and serve Him with all of our hearts, God will bless us, too. Hagar continued to serve God in spite of the painful circumstances. You can, too, if you receive God's miracle of forgiveness and, with His help and love, do your part by forgiving those who have wronged you.

Reflections

Is there someone whom you need to forgive? If so, why?

_____

_____

_____

_____

_____

51

_____

Forgiveness is not easy, but it is possible with God's help. Many people don't deserve to be forgiven, and some people could care less that they have hurt you. But we need to forgive them anyway because, first, God forgives us when we do not deserve it, and second, forgiving others is our only hope for healing the pain we feel.

Roadblocks—

When It Comes to Choice

Part 1

Anorexia Nervosa

by Lisa Spears

As a kid growing up, there was a lot of pressure being put on me to measure up to everyone else's expectations. I always had to look my best, to wear little dresses and be a little lady. As I got older, the pressure to please people only worsened when I noticed how other girls were always comparing themselves to one another. Who had the nicest clothes, who was prettiest, and who was skinniest were constantly talked about in my circle of friends.

At first, I didn't let myself get caught up in the constant competition that went on with the other girls I knew. Before long, however, I found myself becoming preoccupied with how thin I was compared to them. It was more difficult for me when I talked to my mother about my weight concerns. You see, my mother has struggled with her weight all her life. As a young girl, people around her made fun of her. I could see how much it bothered her. I saw her unhappiness with herself, and I worried that I might someday struggle with the same problems.

To make matters worse, I got into a really abusive relationship with a guy who often compared me to thinner girls he'd dated. He made joking comments about my body that made me feel very insecure. I began thinking that my body wasn't pretty and that I needed to lose weight. In reality, I was the right size for my height, but because I felt so bad about myself on the inside, I thought I looked terrible on the outside.

I felt very insecure about myself because I had listened to my boyfriend constantly criticize the way I looked. Then my life took a devastating turn for the worse when the relationship ended, and I found myself alone and empty. I thought that if I didn't do some-thing about my body, if I didn't lose weight, no one else would want to date me.

Because of my insecurities and the inability to control my life, I started starving myself. I never really stopped eating altogether, because if I did, people would catch on to what I was doing. Instead, I ate as little as possible. In fact, every day I ate the same food as the day before. I counted calories and measured every bite. I never let myself eat more than 800 calories a day. I also started working out about three hours a day. I would run four miles or take two aerobics classes in one day because I was so afraid of gaining weight. I worked out so hard and with such intensity that my monthly cycle stopped.

It wasn't long after I started starving myself that I began losing weight. At first I lost five pounds, then another five came off. Before long, I had lost so much weight that my clothes didn't fit me anymore, and I had to buy new ones. I was still not happy with myself, though. When I looked into the mirror, I saw a fat, ugly body when, in truth, there was a skeleton body with no hope for a future staring back at me.

Because I still saw myself as fat, I kept starving myself and working out like crazy. At that time, my weight was about 100 pounds, and

I wore a size 1 in clothes. My skin literally hung off my body, but I didn't see that. My mind was so mixed up because of the hurt I was holding inside that my only way of dealing with it was by starving and exercising.

My parents and friends became very worried about my eating habits. They asked many questions, and some even tried getting me to eat new foods. When they did that, it would frustrate me and cause me to panic because I was desperately afraid of losing control over my body. One time I was in a restaurant with my family and the only thing on the menu that I would eat was oatmeal. When the waitress brought it out, it had butter on it, so I refused to eat it. I was so hungry because I hadn't eaten all day and my mind was tormenting me so much that all I could do was sit there and cry.

That night in the restaurant I saw grief in my parents' eyes. That was when I began to see what I was doing not only to myself, but to them as well. I started realizing that I didn't have to go through the torment in my mind about gaining weight and losing control.

My parents encouraged me to start praying and seeking God to help me through the confusion and panic that controlled me. I went to a pastor in our church for counseling, and he gave me Scriptures to help me. He showed me 1 Peter 5:7 which says, "Cast all your anxiety [cares] on him because he cares for you." I also learned Philippians 4:6 NKJV, "Be anxious for nothing, but in everything with prayer and supplication, with thanksgiving, let your requests be made known to God." Matthew 11:28 was the Scripture I spoke every time I started worrying about my weight: "Come to me, all you who are weary and burdened, and I will give you rest." Before I got out of bed every day, I would say, "God, You are in control of my life, and You love me. You will not let me fail. So, I give my life, my mind, body, and soul to You."

It's been a long and difficult battle for me to overcome the eating disorder anorexia nervosa. I gradually learned to give God control of my thoughts, but it's been very hard. There are still times when the torment in my mind wants to creep back in, but God has given me so much victory as I've learned to trust Him.

I've learned that I have an awesome purpose for my life and that in Christ I am a beautiful creation. I also have so many people in my life who give me a lot of love and encouragement. With the healing and strength I continue to receive from the Lord, each day is a step closer to overcoming.

Reflections

What insecurities and fears led Lisa to begin starving herself? Have you ever struggled with similar insecurities? Write about it.

_____

_____

_____

_____

Why do you think so many young women today struggle with their self-image?

_____

_____

_____

Why do young women spend so much time comparing them-selves to others? Do you struggle with your perception of how you look? Do you constantly compare yourself to others? Why?

_____

_____

_____

Was starvation the answer to Lisa's insecurity problem?

Will starvation and overexercise ever heal a wounded heart, give a young woman the love and acceptance she desperately wants, or draw someone closer to God?

Lisa found her hope and comfort in God's Word. She has been able to fight the battle in her mind using the Sword of the Spirit. (See Eph. 6:17.) You can, too. When you feel overwhelmed, over-burdened, lost, afraid, or out of control, turn to God's Word.

Read Matthew 11:28-30. Write out verse 28:

56

Jesus can give you the rest your mind needs to think clearly and to see truth.

Roadblocks—
When It Comes to Choice

Part 2

The Search for Love:
the Poison Apple

by Shereen Christian

The following is not something that I share with you lightly. In my search for love, I stumbled across a very dark path. I opened a door in my life that almost cost me everything. It started out with a silly little board "game." When I was in junior high school, my girl-friends and I decided to play with a Ouija board. The first time nothing really happened, so we all just giggled about it and went to sleep. That night each one of us was plagued by a nightmare. Little did we know that we had opened a door to the devil.

Later one night at my friend April's house, we pulled out the board "game" again. As we began to "play," an incident took place that almost scared us to death. The weird things that manifested that night continued to happen to us for two years. We quickly put the board away, thinking we'd never, ever pull it out again, but one year later we did. That action led me deeper into the pit. From that point on, I was vulnerable to many different forms of witchcraft: tarot cards, séances, psychics, and "white" magic.

I started reading self-discovery books whose teachings led me astray. Everything I read led me further down the path of destruction. My involvement not only brought disaster into my own life, it affected the lives of my family as well. It was so awful! I can testify to you firsthand that there is nothing cool, nothing safe, and nothing funny about messing around with Ouija boards or anything else along the same lines. They are tools of the enemy to distract you from the path of life. The enemy comes to steal, kill, and destroy! (See John 10:10.)

When these manifestations in my life became so overpowering, I tried to get out. A spirit of suicide fell upon me so heavily one day that I seriously considered taking my own life. That same day, miraculously, a friend invited me to go to church with her. I decided to go, and that decision literally saved me because that Sunday I gave my heart to Jesus.

Here's the scary part: I was only "dabbling" with that board game, the tarot cards, and other evil-related things. I was just playing around, not really taking anything seriously, believing the lie that I was just "exploring." It was only when God delivered me and brought me out of that darkness that I realized how deeply I had fallen in. He brought me up out of that horrible pit into His ever-loving arms.

Reflections

Name some of the ways that the occult or witchcraft has crept into our society.

Can you think of any books, movies, or music that have a hidden meaning or that can draw people into the occult?

_____

_____

How can you help yourself and others avoid this trap?

_____

_____

_____

What does God's Word say?

According to 1 Timothy 4:1-2, should we be careful?

_____

_____

How does 1 John 4:1-6 tell us to test the spirits or recognize the source? _____

_____

_____

In John 10:10, what does the thief, who is our enemy, come to do? _____

_____

_____

Wanted:

A Forever Friend

by Delia Todd

During our lifetime we will develop many friendships. Some will be lasting ones and some may fade away; nevertheless, we should approach each relationship as if it is our only one. Friendships are a necessity in life. Just as the air we breathe sustains us, friendships sustain us—physically, emotionally, and spiritually.

> As iron sharpens iron, so a man sharpens the countenance of his friend.
>
> Proverbs 27:17 NKJV

What qualities do you admire in a friend?

It has been said that a friend is the first person who comes in when the whole world has gone out. We know what we expect from our friends, how we want them to act, and how they should treat us, but we often do not see if we reflect the qualities we demand. Read Proverbs 27:19; this Scripture tells us that where our heart is will reflect who we are.

Do your present friendships reflect the qualities that you admire in a friend? If so, what qualities? _____

_____

_____

_____

Do you reflect the qualities that you admire in a friend?

_____

_____

What changes could you make to be a better friend?

61

_____

_____

Read each verse and write what Solomon had to say about friendship.

Proverbs 11:13 _____

Proverbs 17:17 _____

Proverbs 27:6 _____

Proverbs 27:10 _____

Being a Faithful Friend

The book of Ruth begins with a Hebrew man, Elimelech, who, with his wife Naomi and two sons, had left Bethlehem because of a famine. They lived in Moab, where their sons married Moabite women; one was named Orpah, the other Ruth. Tragedy struck when Elimelech and his two sons died, leaving the women widowed.

Naomi, preparing to return to her homeland, instructed her daughters-in-law to return to their families. After mourning their loss, Orpah obeyed her mother-in-law and returned to her family. Ruth, however, did the unexpected and "clung" to Naomi (1:14).

Read Ruth 1:14-18 and Ruth 2:11-12.

At such a difficult time in Ruth's life, it would have been easy for her to return home to the familiar and seek out a new husband. Instead, Ruth chose to follow and serve her widowed mother.

The Hebrew word for "clung," *dabaq,* means to follow close, to be joined, to keep, and to pursue fervently.[1]

In what ways did Ruth cling and demonstrate friendship-like qualities toward Naomi?

It is clear to see that Ruth had a relationship with God, and her life was under His guidance. She also had a strong commitment to Naomi that only death could separate. Because of her unconditional love for Naomi, Ruth was even willing to travel to an enemy's land where she might not be accepted.

Reflect on a time when you shared a difficult experience with someone.

When Ruth and Naomi arrived in Bethlehem, the women of the town wondered, "Can this be Naomi?" Naomi's response was one of grief and bitterness.

Read Ruth 1:20-21.

How do you think Ruth felt hearing her mother-in-law's response?

_____

_____

_____

Why did Naomi's response not affect Ruth's commitment to her?

_____

The enemy will bring circumstances to friendships that cause hurt feelings, and this could lead to walls being built in our relationships. But as friends we must see beyond the walls and see our need for friendships.

Being faithful in our friendships through love and commitment will produce rewards for all involved. The world in which we live tells us to look out for ourselves, but God asks us to look out for each other. God demands that we remain faithful; to fall short of that would be an injustice to God, our friends, and ourselves.

In Ecclesiastes, Solomon speaks about the rewards of having godly friends. Read Ecclesiastes 4:10-12 and list the mutual benefits.

_____

_____

_____

As believers, we need to examine our relationships and make certain that they reflect God's design for friendships. Are our friendships built on love, faithfulness, commitment, and trust? If not, what can we do to change that? Before we examine our friends and their qualities, we need to look at ourselves. We need to check our hearts, our attitudes, and our actions to make certain that we demonstrate the qualities that Ruth showed towards Naomi.

63

Memorize and commit Ruth 1:16-17 to your heart. The love Ruth had for Naomi is the same love God desires us to have for our friends.

Reflections

Read Proverbs 3:3-4. What does this passage say about relationships? _____

_____

_____

_____

Read Proverbs 21:28. How does this verse relate to friendships?

_____

_____

_____

Seasons of Grace

Part 1

by Erin E. Zonio

I can't remember asking Jesus into my heart as a little girl, but I do remember being very aware of my relationship with Him from an early age. In all the years I have loved Jesus and been a Christian, I've experienced incredible moments with my Savior when I felt like I could reach out and feel His scarred hands. I've also experienced desperate moments when He seemed a million light years away. In my short life, yet comparatively long walk with Jesus, I have learned that there are seasons of grace.

In Ecclesiastes 3, King Solomon begins his famous discourse on the cycle of life:

There is a time for everything, and a season for every activity under heaven:

a time to be born and a time to die, a time to plant and a time to uproot,

a time to kill and a time to heal, a time to tear down and a time to build,

a time to weep and a time to laugh, a time to mourn and a time to dance, a time to scatter stones and a time to gather them, a time to embrace and a time to refrain,

a time to search and a time to give up, a time to keep and a time to throw away,

a time to tear and a time to mend, a time to be silent and a time to speak,

a time to love and a time to hate, a time for war and a time for peace.

As Christians, our lives are not always going to be easy. There will be seasons of joy, seasons of sorrow, seasons of celebration, and seasons of frustration. We haven't been promised comfort, but we have been promised peace. Even when we cannot sense God's Presence, His grace still sustains us.

66

Spiritual Winter

Inevitably, we'll all experience a lifeless time in our walk with the Lord. This is probably the most difficult time in the life of a Christian. "Spiritual winter" can happen as a result of certain events in our life, or it can be because we have become lazy in our service to God. Although we are alive in Christ, we feel dead. He seems far away. We've lost our spiritual hunger. Living for Jesus seems more like a duty than a privilege. We must remember that just because we're having a difficult time *does not mean* we are bad Christians. It means we are ready for growth.

My husband surprised me with a gorgeous poinsettia this past Christmas. It was three individual plants potted as one, making it practically too big to put anywhere! Most of the leaves have now fallen off, and only a few remain on each branch. Yet my beautiful poinsettia is not dying.

During its dormant season, I'll keep the poinsettia in a dark closet. I'll water it regularly, even though it appears to have no life. According to its instructions, if I am faithful to take care of the poinsettia until next October, it will bloom just as beautifully next Christmas as it did this Christmas.

During your apparently dormant season, if you are faithful to continue caring for your soul, watering and nourishing it with the Word, through prayer, and by the Spirit, you will once again bloom. You may feel lifeless inside, but the truth is that this is just a season. There is still life inside you; God is still working in you. Although your "bloom" is gone, life remains.

Have you ever felt like God was distant? Describe that experience in your own words.

_____

_____

_____

Read 1 Peter 5:10 and write it out here:

_____

_____

_____

Cloudy Weather

Oregon is famous for its rainy weather. In the short time we've lived there, we have already noticed that sunny days are few and far between. On most days the sky is gray. In the evenings when I'm driving home from work, it is often difficult to see clearly what is ahead of me. There is either too much fog or too much rain. Sometimes it's scary because I don't know what to expect. If a car were to pull in front of me quickly, I'm not always sure I'd be able to protect myself.

During some seasons of our life, we may not be able to see very far ahead of us. Everything appears foggy, and we are not sure of what's happening around us. It feels dangerous, dark, and lonesome.

Just because we are Christians doesn't mean that we will avoid trouble and suffering. We have an enemy, Satan, who comes to steal, kill, and destroy. (See John 10:10.) Suffering can come in different forms, such as depression, discouragement, boredom, or loneliness. As discouraging as the clouds of suffering are, we can keep in mind that God is still working in us.

God uses times of suffering to refine our faith.

Read 1 Peter 1:6-7. To what is the value of our faith compared?

_____

_____

What happens to our faith as we experience trials, and what is the result? _____

_____

_____

One of my favorite stories is about a man who was visiting a goldsmith. He watched as the man picked up the crucible containing the gold with large tongs, and then held the gold in the middle of the fire. Every few minutes the goldsmith would remove the gold from the fire, look at it, and then place it back in the fire. After watching this routine several times, the visitor asked, "How long do you keep the gold in the fire?"

The goldsmith responded, "Until I can see my face reflected in it."

Although our suffering seems unbearable at the time, as we saw in 1 Peter 6-7, there is a greater plan in progress. God never causes trouble to happen to us; He is always there to help us through it. But His greatest concern is not our contentment with life (although He wants to bless us) but that we are being refined until His image is reflected in us.

You could say that God uses hard times and difficulties to refine us in the same way that we saw the goldsmith refine the gold. Times of suffering that you may experience in your life are opportunities you have to be made more like God.

Reflections

In the past, have you experienced suffering that seemed unending? Describe it.

_____

_____

_____

How did you feel once the suffering was over?

_____

_____

_____

How did it affect your relationship with God?

69

_____

_____

_____

Seasons of Grace

Part 2

by Erin E. Zonio

In the Warmth of the Son

I love being in God's Presence. Whether at home, in my car, or in church, sometimes it seems like nothing else in the world is happening except fellowship with my Father. Sometimes I dance before Him in celebration and sing with my whole heart at the top of my lungs. Other times I bow in humble silence. There is nothing as satisfying and life-giving as the Spirit of God.

This season is often referred to as a "mountain top" experience. You may have experienced it at home as the result of an incredible prayer time, at church after an altar call, or at church camp. When we are "on the mountain," we have the opportunity to view things from God's perspective, rather than just our own. God can teach us amazing things during this season because we are more aware of His activity in our lives.

In the Old Testament, the Israelites built an altar to God when He did something special for them. They viewed the altar as a testimony to God's power and faithfulness. Whenever somebody passed the monument, they were reminded that the God of

Abraham, Isaac, and Jacob was their God and was just as able to come through for them.

Even Noah, who was before Abraham's time, built an altar to the Lord. God had promised He would deliver them and keep them safe during the flood. As soon as the ark landed on dry ground and the animals and people got out, the first thing Noah did was build an altar in honor of God's faithfulness. (See Gen. 8:20.)

We do not build literal altars like that today, but it is a good idea to remember what God does for us. Many people keep a journal and write down the special events in their lives. That way, when they are experiencing a difficult time, they are able to look back and remember exactly what God did for them in the past. Then they are encouraged that He can do the same again.

Describe a time in your life when you felt like God was very close.

71

_____

_____

_____

What do you do to help you remember God's faithfulness in your life? _____

_____

_____

God's Timing

In Ecclesiastes 3:11, after King Solomon described the inevitability of the cycle of life, he came to this conclusion:

He has made everything beautiful in its time....

Sometimes we feel like we have been waiting forever for God to do something new and fresh in our lives, but God still has not responded. While we cannot understand why, we must trust Him and trust His faithfulness. He is at work in a different way than we understand or expect.

> "For my thoughts are not your thoughts, neither are your ways my ways," declares the Lord.
>
> Isaiah 55:8

I have asked God many times to speed things up for me—high school, the days until my driver's test at the DMV, college, getting married. It is difficult for us to wait on God, but it is in these times of waiting that God is able to work a process in us that refines our faith. If we are not patient, we become discouraged and lose hope. Yet, if you have been patient, when the day you've been waiting for arrives, God will have worked all the details out beautifully, and it will be more exciting and fulfilling than you dreamed.

As I said earlier, I have loved Jesus as long as I can remember. I have had the experience of knowing and trusting Him through all different seasons.

When I was in junior high, my relationship with the Lord was very special. I was falling deeper and deeper in love with Him every day. I read the Bible faithfully and would spend hours in my bedroom talking to Him as if I could see Him standing there. My mind was full of questions, and I was hungry to find the answers. I couldn't wait to get to church because I wanted to learn more about Him.

I've also experienced seasons of confusion. When I was a senior in high school, I was dating somebody very seriously, and we were planning on getting married. Without even asking the Lord for wisdom, we got engaged and started planning the wedding. I wanted nothing more than to marry Eric. One time I even told the Lord, "I don't care what You have to say about this!" In my heart I knew marrying Eric wasn't the right thing to do, but I didn't care.

When we broke up, my dreams were crushed. My mother heard me sobbing and held me until dawn as I laid in bed weeping. I didn't believe that I could ever have hope again. I felt like I didn't have anything to live for.

But the Lord came through for me, even though I had turned my back on Him. I was able to go away to college and go on seven missions trips in just four years. I was actively involved in ministry at home and overseas. I remember ministering to young Salvadorans one day and thinking, *If God had allowed me to live life the way I planned it, I wouldn't have the privilege of serving Him like this today.* That summer we saw thousands of children and their parents come to Jesus.

After college, I experienced one of the most difficult times yet. I was in a leadership position where I felt out of place and inadequate. I knew God had called me, but it didn't seem like He had gone with me. I was serving Him and being obedient to Him to the best of my ability, but He seemed more distant than I had ever experienced. I was mean to those I loved, and I wasn't happy with myself. I could only pray that He would grant me His grace and make up for my weaknesses.

Then He brought me to a new place in Him again. He restored me and showed me how I had become stronger because of that difficult situation. God brought me closer to Him, where I felt like He was real again.

In our walk with the Lord, we will go through different seasons.

There will be good times, and there will be hard times. Second Timothy 2:13 says that even if we are *faithless,* he will remain faithful. It is God's very nature to prove Himself to you, to come through for you. God will not let you down. His grace will sustain you. Trust in Him.

Just as my poinsettias are going to bloom beautifully next October, God's timing is perfect, and in His time, He will move beautifully in our lives.

73

Reflections

Are you waiting on God for something? What is it?

_____

_____

What are you doing during this waiting period?

_____

_____

Read Isaiah 40:31. What does God promise us?

_____

_____

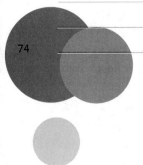

Cling to Purity

by Suzanne Rentz

As I was sitting in a church service one Sunday, the pastor's words kept echoing in my mind: "Cling to purity." I kept thinking, *Yes, we really must cling to purity.*

The world in which we live screams "Compromise!" The colors black and white no longer exist—only multiple shades of gray. To live a pure, holy life, unaffected by the world's influence, we must cling to purity. We must grasp what is pure, never loosening our grip. In this godless generation, cling to purity; it is a life vest keeping you afloat when millions are drowning in their sin.

Purity

The first place we must look is in our heart. Is it pure? During the Middle Ages, when castles were built, their wells were dug in secretive, fortified rooms to protect the castle's supply of fresh drinking water. As we saw earlier, the well was the most crucial part of the whole castle, because if enemy attackers found the well, they could poison the water or cut off its supply, ensuring a quick victory. One of the best-known and wisest kings of Israel was a man named Solomon, who was crowned king at the young age of twenty. He wrote the book of Proverbs in the Bible, and in verse 23, he told us that the heart is the wellspring of life.

Write out Proverbs 4:23.

....

....

If we don't guard our source of continual supply, our heart, our personal enemy, the devil, will pollute it until there is nothing left for us to draw from. If the devil can get to our heart, he can literally destroy us.

In the book of Nehemiah, God spoke to Nehemiah about rebuilding the walls around Jerusalem. At that time, the city was lying in shambles and ruins. Jerusalem was once a strong, beautiful, prosperous city with a pure religion and faith in God. When Jerusalem's enemies destroyed the walls, the battle was over; the enemy had free reign to destroy the city.

76

Picture your heart as Jerusalem. Obviously, the devil is your enemy. The two results of Jerusalem's walls being destroyed were:

1. The enemy devoured and stole treasures or anything of value.

2. The Jews lost their identity and the purity of Jewish culture and religion.

The Jews had to rebuild the walls and guard the city in order to restore Jerusalem to a truly Jewish city.

How do you rebuild the walls around your heart when they are devastated or in shambles? As you read each Scripture below, write down what Nehemiah did to rebuild the walls around Jerusalem.

Nehemiah 2:15-17. *Nehemiah* _____
the damage.

Nehemiah 2:18. *He decided to* _____

....

Nehemiah 4. *When the threats of the enemy came, how did Nehemiah and the Israelites overcome?* _____

....

How can we take what Nehemiah did and apply it to rebuilding the walls around our hearts? _____

_____

_____

_____

Sometimes the walls around our hearts are in good condition. Yet, we must still guard our hearts all the more, knowing that if we give way to compromise and disobedience, we could end up just like Jerusalem. We must cling to purity in our hearts.

Purity in Your Lifestyle

Read 2 Timothy 2:22 and write it out:

_____

_____

_____

Applying this verse to our lives and literally fleeing from youthful lusts is the key to making right choices. The bottom line is, if it glorifies God, go for it; if it doesn't, *stay away!* It is a simple solution if we would just learn to live by that principle.

Let's say you have a friend named Reneé, and she is in the hospital dying of AIDS. A new medicine, which is administered directly into the bloodstream through an IV, has come out which doctors have proven will cure AIDS. Reneé must have this medicine. With it she will live; without it she will die within the next 48 hours.

At the hospital is a man who is wanted on several counts of murder; he is dressed as a doctor. He walks into Reneé's room, and you're standing there by her bed. He wants to switch the medicine for poison by changing the IV. The poison will slowly drip into Reneé's blood stream, and she will die. What would you do? Would you let that happen? Of course you wouldn't. You would make sure her ᴵⱽ stayed hooked up to the good medicine. You would want her to live.

Let's look at this another way. Think of Reneé as being your soul, and the man that is in her hospital room trying to kill her as the devil. What the devil tries to do is take our ᴵⱽ's (what we are hooked up to) out of godly things and plug them into the world. Even if your soul is strong, poison is still poison, and it eventually will kill you—it will just take longer. If you are weak, sick, or in critical condition, the death will come more quickly.

What are examples of "poison" that we can be hooked up to?

Let's take this a step further.

*What are **you** hooked up to?*

Do you need to make some changes? If so, what?

In order to become stronger in the Lord, we must be hooked up to an "ᴵⱽ" such as...

Purity in Relationships

Have you heard the saying, "Friends can make you or break you"? The two most critical and important influences (IV's) that we face as young women are our friendships and our dating relationships. The most common reason Christians lose their relationship with Christ is that they are hanging out with non-Christians or they are dating the wrong men.

Can a relationship be medicine or poison? If so, describe how.

Evaluating Your Relationships

Do your "best" friends encourage, respect, and build you up? Do they help you make the right choices? What do they do when you are down? Do they care? Do they listen and pray?

Do your friends encourage you to do the wrong things? Do they criticize you or discourage your faith in God? When you hang out with them, do you find you always end up in trouble?

Give an example of a bad friendship and what happened in your life as a result of that kind of relationship.

Give an example of a past or present relationship that you know has been a godly friendship.

Men are supposed to be the spiritual leaders in a relationship. Being in a bad relationship is similar to playing with fire. You will get burned when you play with fire—there is no way around it. As surely as you pick up hot charcoal with your hand, it will leave a scar. The first things you will lose are purity and respect.

Read Psalm 37:1-6. Another way you could describe the "safe pasture" this passage mentions is a "secure place away from the dangers of sin" or "making right choices within God's boundaries." God created you, and He knows you better than you know yourself. He gives you the desires of your heart when you "cling to purity" in every area of your life.

Reflections

If you are in a relationship right now, how would you evaluate it?

Roadblocks—
When You Had No Choice

Part 1

Divorce

by Kathy Holt

Shortly after my fourteenth birthday, my whole world came crashing down. It was a beautiful spring day, and I was out playing with my friends when I was asked to come inside. My parents seemed rather somber, and they were sitting on opposite ends of the room. Then the words I never dreamed I would hear came out of my father's mouth. He told us that he loved our mother, but he was in love with another woman and that he and my mother were going to get a divorce. I couldn't believe it! I started crying and so did my mother. I wondered how we were going to make it through this.

It is in times like these that we realize how much we need the Lord to come and make Himself real to us in a way that we have never known. I already struggled with my self-image because my father would pick on the way that I looked by saying, "You are too skinny; stand up straight; you walk funny," and so on. He didn't say it out of malice, but it wounded me just the same. I was told that I looked "wrong" which made me not like myself. After all, if your father doesn't like the way you look, what man will? So now I was dealing with rejection, too.

I felt like my father didn't love me very much or he would have stayed. I think in some ways I determined that I would never again get close to a man; otherwise, he would leave me. After I was old enough to date, this really showed up. I dated many different boys, but I would rarely go out with them more than once. I just wanted to go out and have fun with no commitments.

I was very blessed through the divorce, because I had a father who did not desert me. He was still very much a part of my life, and I saw him regularly. But the pain of the rejection was still present and real. I can remember many times of crying out to the Lord, upset with my life because my parents were divorced. I didn't like seeing them in other relationships because I wanted them back together. Those hopes disappeared when my father married the "other woman." Then I had to deal with feeling that *her* young children replaced me in his life. It was not an easy time, but God was faithful to minister to me when I called on Him.

When I was a senior in high school, I finally got into a steady relationship with a boy, and it was not good. He was very controlling, and I felt trapped. It was only through God's grace that I got out of that relationship, which was leading to marriage. I remember asking God through tears and pain, "What am I going to do now?" He spoke so clearly to my heart that my next step was to go to Bethany College.

God was so good to me through my college years, and I learned so much about Him and His faithfulness. During that time I went through a lot of healing. The Lord helped me to forgive my father for all of the hurtful things that he had said to me and still would say to me. I realized that he didn't understand how his words affected me and that he himself was wounded from his past. I had to renew my mind in the Word and start believing what God said about me instead of what my father was saying.

My earthly father had limitations in his love, but my heavenly Father did not! I was "fearfully and wonderfully" made (Ps. 139:14) exactly the way that would complement my destiny. I began to see myself through God's eyes. I was engraved on the palms of His hands (see Isa. 49:16), and I could not be replaced because I was special to Him.

God promised me that He had a wonderful husband picked out for me and that I didn't need to be afraid. I just needed to listen to Him, trust Him, and follow His leading in my life, knowing that He had my best interest in mind. It happened just as He said. I have a wonderful, godly husband, and we are determined to make our marriage work so our children will not go through what I did. It is not always easy because we are different, but through the Lord, we can and are doing it.

God's Word says that "all things work together for good" (Rom. 8:28 KJV), which doesn't mean that everything that comes our way is good. It simply means that God will take everything, even the bad, and use it for good in our lives. So the divorce that was brought upon me by my parents will be used for good in my life. For one thing I am working hard to make a marriage that will last.

God takes care of us no matter what we are faced with in life. His Word is true. He is faithful and can be trusted to save, deliver, and heal us so we can become like Him.

Reflections

How would you have responded if you were faced with the situation Kathy was? What would you do? What would you say to your parents? How would you "make it through"? (If you have experienced the tragedy of a divorce in your home, really reflect on how you dealt with or are dealing with the situation.)

Kathy said, "I already struggled with my self-image because my father would pick on me." Stop and evaluate how you view yourself. Are you struggling to understand how valuable you are? What role has your father played in your life to shape your self-image? Has he built you up or torn you down?

_____

_____

_____

How did Kathy's situation and relationship with her father affect her relationship with young men? How did they affect her relationship her senior year? How is your relationship with your father affecting your dating standards and choices?

_____

_____

Whose voice are you listening to and believing? Do you realize how much God cherishes you? Suggestion: Write a prayer to God asking Him to reveal to you His everlasting love and commitment to you, and to help all things in your life to work together for good.

_____

_____

_____

_____

Roadblocks—
When You Had No Choice

Part 2

Depression: Road to Recovery

by Rebecca Harrison

In my room is where I spent much of my time as a teenager, talking to friends but never really getting anywhere in my head—same old thoughts; same old feelings. Of course, I really loved Jesus and thought I knew Him, but everything still seemed so hard.

So many nights I'd lie awake for hours; my thoughts just wouldn't stop. Sometimes I would find "pictures" of faces in the texture of my painted wall hovering by my bed. Time passed, but barely. Still, awake, exhausted, eventually drifting off to some form of sleep.

The "haunting" of my mind (filled with negative thoughts) shot arrows through my head of inadequacy, feelings of "less than," insecurity, and fear. The arrows chased me down wherever I went, always willing to add one more wound. Hurts began to mount; depression was close behind.

After all, my own birth mother had given me up; never mind that I had good parents now. After all, I wasn't as good as "you know who," who had seemingly every talent known to man. Never mind that I played the piano, won a talent contest, and performed on television. After all, I wasn't very outgoing like so many others (or so I thought). I knew how to be by myself; never mind that I had many great friends. After all, I always felt just one step behind in school; never mind that I was in the honor society. After all, I didn't have "him." After all, if I just stopped eating, I'd be thinner like "her." After all, I had bad hair days every day—and on and on it went.

The roadblocks were many. Growing up was hard. Talking to the Lord was what I did a lot. *Lord, how do I get rid of these thoughts, all the hurts and pain?* I'd gone to church my whole life. I'd memorized Scripture. I'd been a "good girl," no drugs, alcohol, or sex here. Those weren't things that snared me. But the battle of the mind—that should be a snap to fix. After all, it wasn't a thing anyone could see.

I was kind of quiet and shy, kept my opinions to myself; after all, who wanted to hear what I had to say? It was easy to let others run right over me, very easy. I was good at staying lost in my own mind maze. It was painfully comfortable there. It was a place I knew well.

Life proceeded—getting married at nineteen years old had its ups and downs, and the battle in my mind continued. If I were just a better wife, things would be better and he would love me more. If I were just a better wife...if I could just stop all this thinking...if....

Fear began to be my constant companion. It is an animal that feeds on itself. It starts out very innocently, very small. It takes on many different masks—*What if he quit loving me...what if he found someone else...what if someone came and took my kids....* Panicked, I bolted the doors and hid cowering in a corner of the laundry room. Leftover pain pills I took seemed to dull the ache enough to leave me displayed on the couch like a zombie. My friend came and prayed for me. I couldn't pray. The only feeling I knew was fear and pain.

Breakout

How could I get out of this dark prison? *Help, Lord!* It felt as if I were drowning and bobbing up and down trying to get breaths of air. The fierce waves had just about consumed me. I felt as though I were trying, with all my might, to get one last breath before I went under for the last time.

I knew Jesus was the *only* way out. I knew I had two children who needed me to be all right. I had to try everything I could to get better, with the Lord's help. So, I did the only thing I knew to do. I went to the Word. I read all the Scriptures I could find on fear. I remembered the Scriptures I had memorized as a child and said them often. I read the Word. I thought about the Word. I prayed. I listened for God to speak to me through the Word to my heart.

I was nestled in a cocoon of isolation. I had withdrawn from most people around me. I was tired of trying to explain what I couldn't understand. I was tired of just looking at people and the tears coming. I was numb on the inside. I knew I had to get out and be with people who loved God, but I didn't feel like it. I didn't want to, but I forced myself. I began going to a woman's Bible study. And wouldn't you know, they were going through the Word and studying a book that dealt with emotional healing. God's always one step ahead, isn't He?

My fragmented thoughts had to be gathered. The depression and unrelenting negative thoughts would come. They had to go, but it seemed as if they had grown quite accustomed to their "home." I had to "clean house," but every time I tried to think of something else, my mind would do a U-turn. Surely crazy couldn't be far away.

I knew I had to physically do something, so when the arrows came, I would find an activity that would take my mind off of what it was dwelling on. It was a conscious choice. (See Isa. 7:15; 2 Cor. 10:5.)

87

I needed friends; the ones I'd had were pushed to the background, but I needed and received their prayers and support and love. I began going to a counselor to reinforce what the Lord had begun to change in me, regardless of my feelings. I was out in the wide open with Jesus—no more hiding or running. It was time to face the fears, no matter what the cost.

Soon I found that a lack of forgiveness can put you in your own prison, that bitterness will keep you there, and that God's forgiveness was the key to unlocking that prison. (See Ps. 146:7.) I learned that the hands of my heart could be so tightly wrapped around the past hurts that only Jesus could uncurl my grip. I learned to think (meditate) on the Word and the goodness of God. (See Josh. 1:8; Phil. 4:8.) I learned how to apply the Word to my daily life. (See Prov. 22:17; 2 Tim. 2:7.)

88

I learned that Jesus was the One who gave me my identity. He had made me His daughter. (See Eph. 1:5.) My name was engraved on His hands. (See Isa. 49:16.) I learned that He had known me from the beginning. He had made me in my mother's womb. (See Ps. 139:13-15.)

I learned that He desires me to have truth (His Word) in my innermost parts and that knowing the truth will set me free. (See Ps. 51:6; John 8:32.) I learned that I am not a slave to fear and that God has not given me a spirit of fear, but instead, He has given me a spirit of power, love, and a sound mind. (See Rom. 8:15; 2 Tim. 1:7.) I learned that He never changes (see Heb. 13:5) and that what Satan wanted to use to ruin me, God used for good. (See Gen. 50:20.) When I am weak, it is He who is my strength. (See 2 Cor. 12:9,10.) He has plans to give me a hope and a future. (See Jer. 29:11-14.)

Freedom: One Way

So a new path was before me. Each day brought choices. Decisions had to be made before the choices were even an option.

I had decided not to mediate on the things I used to but, instead, think on things that were good. I decided to forgive immediately. I decided to renew my mind by letting the Word change me. (See Rom. 12:2.) I decided to be with God's people. I decided to open up to safe people who loved me. I decided to just try, and if I failed, so what—Jesus never stops loving me. I decided to think soberly of myself, not too highly and not too lowly. (See Rom. 12:3.) I decided to put on Jesus' attitudes first. I decided to be thankful for everything. (See Eph. 4:20.) I decided to comfort others with the comfort He has given me. (See 2 Cor. 1:4.)

Time has passed. I have a better relationship with my Lord and Savior. I see His love for me daily. I am humbled by His grace in my life, and I am awed by His compassion and care for me. I am amazed by His boundless mercy. I have come to realize that the journey will not be without turbulence, nor will every day be a bed of roses. Life is not without pain. But that's okay. Sometimes, when I see fear try to creep back in, I know that it is a little sign that I need to get back on the right track. Jesus is always with me, and I can never be separated from His love, not even for a moment. (See Rom. 8:35-39.) He has begun a good work in me and will continue. (Phil 1:6.)

89

> You have turned for me my mourning into dancing; You have loosed my sackcloth and girded me with gladness,
> That my soul may sing praise to You and not be silent. O Lord my God, I will give thanks to You forever.
>
> Psalm 30:11,12 NASB

Reflections

Can you relate to the "battle of the mind" that Rebecca wrote of? If so, what do you find yourself dwelling on, being bogged down with? _____

_____

_____

Do you ever play the "If only..." and "What if..." game? Read Philippians 4:11. What do you think the apostle Paul meant by "I have learned the secret of being content"?

What "if only's" and "what if's" do you need to give up in order to be content? Commit them to the Lord right now.

Rebecca said, "A lack of forgiveness can put you in your own prison, that bitterness will keep you there." Are you failing to forgive someone who has hurt or disappointed you?

Stop and honestly evaluate how that lack of forgiveness is affecting your life. Write about the situation you are struggling with, and as you write, give your pain to Jesus. Ask Him to help you to forgive the person or persons who have caused your fear and pain. When you finish writing, don't allow your mind to replay the hurt anymore. Every time it "pops into your head," remind yourself and the enemy (Satan) that you have forgiven that person.

_____

_____

How did the Word of God help Rebecca in her healing process? Do you think it can help you?

_____

_____

_____

_____

Roadblocks —

When You Had No Choice

Part 3

Sexual Abuse

by LaFaye Tapper

Sometimes we go through hard situations and we don't always understand why. You may be going through a difficult experience right now, and you have no idea why you have to endure this pain in your life. But I can assure you that the deeper the valley you are stumbling through, the higher will be the mountain top when you reach it, if you will keep your eyes on God.

Sometimes God delivers us out of situations right away. Other times, He goes through them with us. (See Ps. 23:4.) But either way, His love is everlasting, and He is always a very present help in time of trouble. (See Ps. 46:1.)

Learn to seek God's help and guidance, especially in facing and overcoming any hurts in the past that may have you bound. Bondage steals our joy. Our precious Lord can break the bonds that our enemy, Satan, tries to reinforce. Claim for yourself your blessing. And always remember, "…greater is He that is in you, than he that is in the world" (1 John 4:4 KJV).

It has been more than thirteen years since I first began to face my pain. I am going to share my story with you because I believe that God can heal you of any emotional and spiritual hurts through my testimony of the suffering and healing that He has brought to me.

When my mother was only thirteen years old, her father (my grandfather) died, leaving behind my grandmother, my mother, and her two brothers. About two years later, my grandmother remarried. Her new husband seemed to be a very nice man who wanted to be a good husband and father. They went to church together and out to dinner and the movies, and my grandmother believed that she had found someone who could at least partially fill the emptiness in their lives. But things were not as they seemed to be.

Shortly after the marriage, they learned that this new person in their family was an alcoholic. And he wasn't a "happy drunk." When he was drinking, he was *mean!* For several years the marriage was stormy, filled with separations and attempts at divorce. Finally, after a long separation, he begged to come back and promised that he would change. For all appearances, their life was much better.

About three years after my grandparents' reconciliation, I was born. My parents had moved back to Baton Rouge and lived only a few blocks from my grandparents. My grandmother was very close to my older brother, and my grandfather favored me. He was a fun grandfather, and I loved being with him.

When I was about two years old, my grandfather began to sexually abuse me. At this young age, I didn't realize that what he was doing was wrong. I really didn't even understand what was happening to me. The abuse continued for several years, but I thought that this was normal behavior and never told anyone what he was doing.

But as I grew older, I began to realize that this was wrong. I began to fear being around my grandfather. I didn't want to go to my grandmother's house at all. I avoided him totally, but I never

93

told anyone why. I did not know of his alcoholism and abusive behavior that my mother and grandmother had suffered in the early years of the marriage. But still, I kept my secret locked away.

When I was a teenager, I began dating a young man from my church. One night as we watched a movie together, something in the movie triggered my suppressed pain, and I began to cry, sobbing uncontrollably. Of course, he didn't understand; *I* didn't even understand.

Two weeks later, depression struck. I cried over everything and nothing. No one could understand this drastic change in my personality—from happy-go-lucky to total sadness. I couldn't eat. I couldn't sleep. I lost fourteen pounds in two weeks. In desperation, my mother took me to our family physician. His diagnosis was that physically I was in good health, but that I was suffering from depression. He suggested that I receive counseling.

94

During the first month of my depression, I could do nothing more than pray. I had given my heart to Jesus when I was seven years old. I slept with my Bible under my pillow at night. I was so desperate for God to deliver me from this darkness, this heaviness, this cloud of gloom hanging over my heart that would not lift.

Then one day I received a word from the Lord while reading my Bible. "But now, thus says the Lord…'Fear not, for I have redeemed you; I have called you by your name; you are Mine. When you pass through the waters, I will be with you; and through the rivers, they shall not overflow you. When you walk through the fire, you shall not be burned, nor shall the flame scorch you'" (Isa. 43:1,2 NKJV).

This said to me that we may feel like we're drowning in our circumstances, but He promises us that we won't. We may feel like we're going to be incinerated because the situation is so difficult, but He promises us that the flame won't even scorch us. Truly, our Lord works in mysterious ways. This verse from Isaiah was the beginning of my healing.

Another verse, Psalm 51:6 NASB, became the foundation in my search. "Behold, You desire truth in the innermost being, And in the hidden part You will make me know wisdom." God began to open my "Pandora's box" of hidden pain and gently compelled me to face each one.

Eventually, my grandfather died of cancer, but although I was concerned for his soul, I had never really forgiven him for what he did to me. Yet, God commanded me to forgive him (see Matt. 6:15), and several years after he died, I did stand at the altar of forgiveness. I could not allow this anger to stand between my Lord and me.

Our God is faithful. What He promises in His Word, He will perform. He used the people closest to me to help me learn of the constancy of His love. I was baptized in (or filled with) His Holy Spirit, an experience that changed my whole life for the better. (See Acts 1:7; 2 Cor. 6:16 KJV.) My "new-found" joy began to blossom and grow into full bloom. And God will do the same for you. If you haven't already done so, I encourage you to invite Him into your heart, allow Him to guide you, and accept the love, peace, joy, and forgiveness He offers.

95

Reflections

LaFaye was forced to conceal her grandfather's sin. As she grew up, the burden of keeping the secret ate away at her on the inside. Are you hiding a secret that you feel is too awful to reveal? What is it? Ask God to help you to face your secret pain so He can heal you. If you are presently in an abusive situation, seek help immediately! _____

_____

_____

_____

As LaFaye suffered depression, what finally provided help and comfort to her? All the instruction, comfort, direction, and inspiration we need for our lives are found in God's Word. Make a commitment today to read it, study it, meditate (think) on it, and memorize it. Your fear and pain will vanish as you do.

Write out Matthew 6:15.

_____

_____

_____

LaFaye's greatest challenge may have been to forgive her grandfather. She wrote, "I could not allow this anger to stand between me and my Lord." What, if any, unforgiveness is standing between you and your Lord? Write a letter to whomever you are struggling to forgive. Ask God to help you to forgive that person today.

_____

_____

_____

_____

_____

96

If you or someone you know has been or is being abused, to whom should you go for help?

_____

_____

_____

Roadblocks—
When You Had No Choice

Part 4

Adoption: Disappointment or Divine Appointment

by Judy Rentz

"Mommy, what does 'adopted' mean?" asked my six-year-old daughter, Jordyn, one night while watching the movie *Annie*. All these years later my mind goes back to the phrases I heard over and over as a little girl: "We chose you" and "God gave you to us." Such simple phrases, but they catch the very heart of a miracle in my life—the miracle of adoption. I stand strong and secure today because I decided to accept the fact that God *did* give me to my wonderful parents, they *did* choose me, and, in fact, God *chose me.* Amazing!

The Bible tells us that children are a gift from the Lord. This defines the very essence of adoption—we were a gift from God to our parents, a reward. (See Ps. 127:3.) Yet, adopted children often struggle with feelings of rejection, loneliness, confusion, and fear.

As a young girl, I made a choice to have victory over these feelings and not let them define me. I made choices on how I would think and what I would believe by standing on the Word of God. Second Corinthians 10:3-5 says, "For though we live in the world, we do not wage war as the world does. The weapons we fight with are not weapons of the world. On the contrary, they have divine power to demolish *strongholds.* We demolish arguments and every pretension that sets itself up against the knowledge of God…."

Basically, what all that means is that we find Scriptures to fight the battles in our minds. We let God tell us who we are and what we are worth, not our circumstances. And we make a choice to believe Him.

You Have a Choice To Make.

Second Corinthians 10:5 instructs us to take captive every thought to make it obedient to Christ. Let's look at some of the issues that you might be battling (if you are adopted), what God says about them, and the choices you must make.

Issue #1: "I was rejected."

Reality is that the day my unwed, teenage, biological mother found out she was pregnant with me was undoubtedly the darkest day of her life. I am sure she cried, probably wished she would miscarry, and possibly contemplated abortion. I know that my conception brought about tremendous grief in her life.

Does that hurt me? *Absolutely not,* because on the other hand, I know of the long, lonely years of childlessness that my parents endured. I have heard of the despair and disappointment when the doctor told my mother, "You'll never be able to have children." Then, I hear of the wonderful, exciting day when I was placed in their empty arms when I was three weeks old. Their feelings of fulfillment seem beyond description. So I made a choice; I wasn't a problem—I was an answer!

That is what it means in the Bible to take your thoughts "captive" to "demolish arguments." You make the choice to believe whether you were a disappointment or a divine appointment, whether you were rejected or received, discarded or desired. To your parents you were the fulfillment and the completion of their hearts' desire.

Issue #2: "I was unwanted."

You must realize the pressure that your biological mother was under and that she probably had three choices.

1. Abort you.

2. Have you, keep you, and raise you in a single-parent home. Often this means she would have to go to work and put you in full-time daycare or go on welfare in order to stay home.

3. Place you in a loving home with people who have prayed and prepared for a precious baby.

I know that my biological mother chose the most difficult path for her, and I am grateful. She did not choose a "quick end." The heartache of letting me go must have been terrible, but she gave me the most precious gift—a whole family. She chose life for me. Deuteronomy 30:19 has a unique meaning to me. It says, "…Now choose life, so that you and your children may live." The verse actually refers to choosing to serve God, but to me, it always represented what my birth mother did for me: She chose life that I might live!

You may be saying, "That's all great and fine, but I really wasn't wanted. My biological parent walked away." My husband, Eddie, was also adopted, but with much different circumstances. His birth father walked away when Eddie was a baby, and he's only seen him three times in his whole life. That was his father's choice. But the wonderful thing is that he was wanted and adopted by another man, Harry Rentz, who raised him and gave him his name and a

99

family. Eddie was wanted! If this happened to you, you must make a choice not to focus on the one who walked away, but on the one who welcomed you into his heart.

Issue #3: "History will repeat itself."

When I was a little girl, my father went to a conference where a well-known speaker advised against adoption because the "sins of the father are passed down to the child." Needless to say, my father left the conference! But how does that idea affect us as adopted children? Does that mean we will do as our biological parents did? Will I be sexually promiscuous? Will Eddie walk away from his family? Will history repeat itself?

First of all, you must realize that ultimately *sin is your choice.* No one can make you sin, and you are not genetically disposed to specific sins. True, we do all sin, as Romans 3:23 says, "for all have sinned and fall short of the glory of God." However, Eddie cannot walk away from his family and claim, "My birth father made me do it." We are responsible for the choices we make. If you have accepted Jesus into your heart, 2 Corinthians 5:17 says, "Therefore, if anyone is in Christ, he is a new creation; the old has gone, the new has come!"

You are a new creation, and when you accept Jesus as your Lord and Savior, you have a new nature—His nature.

You do not need to be fearful. Romans 8:12-17 says we are not slaves to fear because we have received the spirit of sonship; we are God's children. As children, we are heirs, and as "heirs of God," we are "co-heirs with Christ." We are uniquely qualified to understand that God has adopted us as His children!

If you and your family do believe there are some generational issues to be addressed, I recommend talking with your pastor or youth pastor. They can help your family by asking the Lord to break ungodly ties and inheritances and asking the Father to seal those areas in your life. Matthew 16:19 and 18:18 tell us that whatever is bound in heaven will be bound on earth. Seek spiritual guidance and counsel in this area. Your pastors are there to help you in your spiritual walk with God.

Issue #4: "I was an accident and, therefore, have no real purpose in life."

You may have been a surprise to your biological parents, but you certainly weren't a surprise to God. Psalm 139:15-16 says, "My frame was not hidden from you [God] when I was made in the secret place. When I was woven together in the depths of the earth, your [God's] eyes saw my unformed body. All the days ordained for me were written in your book before one of them came to be."

Isn't it amazing that with everything going on in the world, God saw "little ol' you" and made a place for you? You are important to God. You are special and unique, indeed! When you hear that God cares about the sparrow and knows the number of hairs on a person's head, you can know it to be true because of what He did in your life! (See Matt. 10:29,30.)

In Jeremiah 29:11 God tells us that He has plans for us, "...plans to prosper you and not to harm you, plans to give you hope and a future." No matter the circumstances under which you were conceived or who is raising you now, God knows about you and has had plans for you since before you were born. You were not an accident to Him! Remember, all things work together for good for those who are called according to His plan. (See Rom. 8:28.)

Issue #5: "What should I do about finding my biological parents?"

This is a very individual choice. I have an opinion, but this is ultimately between you and your parents. I am a firm believer of not finding your biological parents. They made the choice to give you as normal a life as possible. The Lord has blessed you with a family that loves you. I believe it best to leave it that way. You never know what you will find or who will be hurt; many times *you* are the one who gets hurt.

I do believe that you should pray for them if you think of them. You could pray that the Lord will heal their hearts, that they will come to know Jesus and will have fulfilled lives.

I like what Jeremiah 33:6-9 says when I think of and pray for my biological parents.

> "… I will heal my people and will let them enjoy abundant peace and security. I will bring Judah and Israel back from captivity and will rebuild them as they were before. I will cleanse them from all the sin they have committed against me and will forgive all their sins of rebellion against me. Then this city will bring me renown, joy, praise and honor before all nations on earth that hear of all the good things I do for it; and they will be in awe and will tremble at the abundant prosperity and peace I provide for it.'"

102

Issue #6: "How do I fight these thoughts on a daily basis?"

If you find that a war wages in your mind and emotions, stand on the Word of God. In other words, hold on to Scriptures that discuss this, such as 1 Corinthians 2:16 and Philippians 4:8. And make the Word the final word in your life. I urge you to commit some of these verses to memory. Write them out, put them on your mirror, refrigerator, or computer, someplace where you'll see them regularly. When you struggle, remind yourself that you are:

Chosen by God

A gift from God

Called by God

Loved by God

Able to do all things through Christ

A new creation

Redeemed, blessed, holy, and sanctified

Accepted

And always remember: *Your parents are God's gift to you.*

They longed for you, prayed for you, and rejoiced the day the Lord gave you to them.

Most of all, they will love you forever!

Reflections

Judy chose to learn to "stand on the Word of God" at an early age. What does that mean, and what difference can the Word of God make in our lives?

While you may not have been adopted, you may struggle with some of the "issues" Judy wrote about. What five "issues" did she write about, and have you found yourself dealing with any of them?

At the end of Judy's testimony, she listed eight things that God's Word says about you. Break out your Bible and find verses to support these statements. (Hint: Use the concordance at the back of your Bible.)

Chosen by God _____

A gift from God _____

Called by God _____

Loved by God _____

Able to do all things through Christ _____

A new creation _____

Redeemed, blessed, holy, and sanctified _____

Accepted _____

What words of encouragement can you share with a friend who is having a hard time dealing with the fact that he/she is adopted?

_____

_____

_____

_____

Free To Love

by Erin E. Zonio

One way to love others freely is by staying free from envy. By not looking at ourselves and others and then weighing the differences, we are free to love. That comes from recognizing that God has abundantly gifted us in very special ways, as He has done for others.

I have a friend whom I could have lost due to comparison, if God had not intervened. Our friendship started out very simple. I met Jennifer my first week in college, and for a week, a whole group of us did everything together: We ate all our meals together, we went on scavenger hunts together, and we prayed together. Jennifer led us around our new home and introduced us to new sites, helping us to become more comfortable in the new world of college.

A few months later, my friendship with Jennifer took on a new dimension. She started attending the church in which I had grown up. It was great to have a college friend at my church, and now I could show her the way around *my* world. Soon, however, I began to envy her. Everybody adored her. People I had worked so hard at being friends with just naturally flocked to her. She stole the crowd's attention when she walked into a room. Effortlessly, she won the hearts of everyone in our congregation.

It was not long until I began to resent her. *Why does everybody like her so much? What does she do that I can't do? Who is she, anyway, coming in here and changing the way things are? I'm supposed to be everybody's sweetheart, not her!* I got tired of hearing everybody talk about her, and I even began to gossip about her to others.

One day, I went to lunch with a group of friends. Jennifer was not able to go, so I was relieved. However, it did not mean her influence was not there.

"Did you hear what Jennifer did? She's so funny!" *Here we go again,* I thought.

"She's got a personality and a half!"

"She's the most wonderful thing that's happened to our church!" "We *love* Jennifer!"

I couldn't stand it anymore, and I blurted out, "She's not perfect, you know!"

Suddenly everybody got quiet and looked my way. Too humiliated to say anything, I looked back down at my plate and started stuffing my red face with my lunch.

How do you think I treated Jennifer when I saw her? I was polite, but I certainly was not gracious or loving. I had become so envious of her that I began to resent her and think badly of her. This resentment could have eventually eaten away at me and could have led me to be mean to her. Fortunately, God intervened. I was able to let go of the feelings I had towards her, even to the point that she was a bridesmaid in my wedding recently, and soon I will be a bridesmaid in hers.

Comparing myself with Jennifer caused me to criticize her. It started out in my heart, then it crept out in the form of gossip. I also felt like I was in competition with her. If she got more attention from a crowd, then I was losing. I *had* to keep up with her, if not beat her. I *had* to be more special than her. What allowed our friendship to grow was that God helped me see how much He values me and how much He values Jennifer. He loves and cherishes both of us. I do not need to feel insecure about myself when I see her succeed.

What about people we think are not as good as we are?

We may not want to admit it, but we look down on others at times, whether because of the clothes they wear, the way they talk, or who their friends are. This is still comparing ourselves to other people, and it still leads to judging them. Again, the result is that we do not demonstrate to them the grace of God as it was meant to be demonstrated. We begin to criticize and make fun of them. We make them feel unimportant. God, however, tells us that we should honor one another above ourselves. (See Rom.12:10.) He is shaping and molding each of us into the individuals He created us to be. The common thread we all should have is reflecting the character of His Son Jesus.

If we can keep that in mind, then there is no reason to feel like we need to be better than others. We just need to be who God desires us to be.

Is there someone to whom you often compare yourself?

107

_____

_____

_____

How do you feel about yourself when you think about him/her?

_____

_____

_____

Describe your attitude toward that person.

_____

_____

_____

Do you demonstrate grace to him/her? _____

_____

_____

Ask God to set you free from the destructive habit of comparing yourself to people. Ask Him for forgiveness. He wants you to be free to enthusiastically and sincerely share His grace with others.

Acceptance

People do amazing things for acceptance. Some people wear the right clothes just to be accepted. Others pierce all sorts of odd places on their bodies simply for acceptance. I've flipped through television channels and have seen people who actually undergo surgery to have implants in their scalp so they can screw spikes into their head! Ouch! I've also seen nose rings attached to chains that are attached to another part of their body.

108

From tattoos to body piercings, styles have become outrageous. People adopt these styles to be cool and to gain acceptance because deep down, everyone longs to be accepted.

How do you define acceptance? _____

_____

When I think of acceptance, I think of the word "freedom"— freedom to be who I really am; freedom for God to work out His plan in me; freedom from insecurity; freedom from others' opinions; freedom from intimidation, envy, criticism, and comparison.

All this freedom is found when we become a Christian. God, by His grace, floods us with His love and acceptance. If there's anywhere a person can find the acceptance they are searching for, it should be among Christians.

Offering Acceptance

My sister, Sarah, was born before my third birthday. We played well together for several years, but when I was eight years old, I began to resent her. I wanted nothing to do with her. She really did not do anything wrong, except "little sister" things, but she just bugged me. If I told somebody my favorite car was a navy blue BMW 325i convertible with gray interior, I would soon hear her tell her friends that *her* favorite car was a navy blue BMW 325i convertible with gray interior. It drove me crazy!

Eventually, I began to despise her more and more. I did not want her to invade any of *my* world. My friends could not be her friends. If I was watching television with our family and she walked in to join us, I would leave the room. I avoided sitting next to her at the dinner table, but if I could not get out of it, I would eat my dinner quickly so I could "go back to my homework" just to get away from her.

I did not enjoy resenting Sarah, but it had taken such root in my heart that I could not change anything. I went to the altar at church week after week all through high school, asking God to change my heart and to give me genuine love for my sister. Finally, after attending a Daughters of Heaven Ministries Conference, I was ready to hear God speaking to my heart, and soon after, He did.

He told me that the reason I could not love Sarah was because I did not base her value on how our heavenly Father saw her, but on how I saw her. In order to love her, I needed to see how valuable she was to God. At the same time, I needed to understand how valuable I was to God, not based on my performance as a believer, but simply as His daughter.

In time, I learned that God loves me no matter what, and then I began to see that God loves Sarah no matter what, too. An appreciation for the grace He had extended to me caused me to be able to love and value Sarah.

I have learned to accept Sarah, and now she is my friend. I love her because I see how much God loves her. Yes, as my sister, she has failed me at times, but I know that God is working in her life and shaping her into the character of His Son, just as He is with me and with all who believe.

God has accepted me by His grace. I cannot help but accept those around me.

Reflections

We saw in an earlier entry that grace can be described as something given to or done for someone without expecting anything in return. How is acceptance an example of grace?

_____

_____

_____

What is one way you can use grace to show acceptance to someone you know?

_____

_____

_____

Leave Your Baggage Behind

Part 1

Disappointment

by Kim Clements

Have you ever really hoped for something only to be faced with utter disappointment when you realized that things weren't going to work out as you thought they would? Disappointment is something we all must learn how to handle. It is an unavoidable part of life. The fact is that none of us can have *everything*, go *everywhere*, and do *everything* that we want. No matter how carefully we plan our lives or how diligently we serve the Lord, as long as we live in an imperfect world inhabited by imperfect people, we will at one time or another come face to face with disappointment.

Name a time that you faced a disappointing situation.

_____

_____

_____

Disappointment is one thing that has destroyed more lives than just about anything else. It can crush young people to the point that they will actually turn their backs on God. This is how it happens.

When God doesn't answer their prayers, especially the really major ones like, "How come my parents got divorced even though I prayed that they wouldn't?" or "Why didn't I get that leadership position I really wanted?" they become angry with God. Or if God doesn't give them an immediate answer to their questions, they stand bewildered, unable to function until they get their questions answered. Again, they become angry with God.

Then, the enemy, Satan himself, begins to spread his propaganda. He whispers lies in the form of thoughts in their mind, saying, "See, there is no God," or "If God really loved you He would give you what you want," or "Why do you even call yourself a Christian? You can't even get your prayers answered!" If they don't, at that moment, choose to trust God, then Satan has successfully paved the way for doubt and bitterness, and they begin their journey away from God.

Before they realize it, they have completely distanced themselves from God. All they have with them are some distorted memories about what they were upset about in the first place and a lot of emotional baggage that is much too heavy to carry. Dazed, bitter, and confused, they wonder what happened and how they got where they are.

Have you ever felt frustrated because you felt like God wasn't answering your prayers fast enough or in the way you wanted Him to? _____ Yes _____ No

If you answered "yes," write about what happened and how you handled it. _____

_____

_____

Read Isaiah 55:8-9 and 2 Peter 3:8. What do these verses tell you about God and how He answers our prayers?

Often we have little control over whatever situation brings the disappointment our way, but we always have control over how we will respond to the disappointment. If we choose to give our hurt and disappointment to the Lord, He will replace our pain with comfort and will lead us in His divine plan for our lives. If we choose to bury our pain or take it out on others, our lives will end in destruction. The choice is ours. The choice is yours.

113

Write out 1 Peter 5:7.

The word "care" in this verse and context refers to any distractions, anxieties, burdens, and worries that we experience in our everyday lives. Our heavenly Father didn't design us to carry around a bunch of hurt, worry, and disappointment, but so many people do. It's like the tourist who packs way too much while on vacation.

I have a friend who came back from her trip overseas with twice as much stuff as she had when she left. She could hardly carry her things through the airport. She kept dropping her bags, and finally one of them ripped. When they announced that the plane she was scheduled to fly on had mechanical difficulty and that the passengers would have to board a different plane on the other side of the airport, she just about totally lost control emotionally. Really, she was carrying too much.

Many young women are needlessly carrying around so much emotional baggage that totally losing control is just around the corner for them. Unlike carrying too much baggage at the airport, they can't just whip out $1.50 for a luggage cart to haul all of their pain and disappointment around. And they think that they have to carry it themselves. But, remember, God tells us in His Word to cast *all* our cares on Him because He cares for us. Giving your disappointment to God means you can leave your emotional "baggage" behind.

Reflections

Are you carrying around a bunch of "baggage"? Take a moment to examine your heart. Read Psalm 139:23-24. Ask the Holy Spirit to show you what's in your "suitcase," and use the lines below to confess what you have discovered there.

Leave Your Baggage Behind

Part 2

Disappointment

by Kim Clements

In Judges 13 we read about a man named Manoah who had a wife but no children. Manoah's wife was the woman that the Bible never mentioned by her own name, but Hebrew tradition says that she was a godly woman during a time in Israel's history when few godly women could be found. We don't know much about her. The only thing we know for sure is that she was barren, unable to have children.

Being barren was just about the most difficult and disappointing thing that a woman in those days had to face. Women found their sense of value and worth from raising children. Month after month she must have suffered great disappointment when her monthly cycle came, bringing the verdict that she was still not pregnant, that she would not become a mother. If any woman deserved to have a baby, it was Manoah's wife.

One day an angel appeared to her and said, "Indeed now, you are barren and have borne no children, but you shall conceive and bear a son" (v. 3 NKJV). Manoah's wife had suffered greatly and now her pain was going to come to an end. Why didn't God answer her prayers and give her a child when she wanted one?

Remember, Isaiah 55:8-9 and 2 Peter 3:8 tell us that God's ways are not our ways, and His timing is different than ours. God's plans for Manoah's child were great, and His timing in bringing this special baby into the world was perfect. God had allowed Manoah's wife to remain barren so that when she finally became pregnant and gave birth, everyone would know that it was a miracle from God and would understand how special baby Samson was.

Did you say Samson, you may be thinking, *the Samson who was used by God to deliver Israel from the oppression of the Philistines?* Yes, Manoah's wife was Samson's mother.

Sometimes God says no to our prayers because He has a higher purpose for us than our limited imagination can understand. Manoah's wife, Samson's mother, had her greatest desire delayed so that God's highest purpose and plan could be worked out in her life. We need to remember that when God says no, it is for a very good reason.

As we continue to look at the story of Samson's mother, we can learn some practical tips to help us deal with our own disappointments.

1. She didn't lose her hope and faith in God. (See Judg. 13:6,7.)

When the angel of the Lord came to her and said that she would bear a son, she readily accepted the news. She didn't doubt that God was answering her prayer but went straight to her husband to tell him what the angel had said.

If you give up your hope and faith in God, you won't recognize His answer when it comes. You will be too bogged down after dragging your "baggage" all over the place. Remember, no matter what disappointments come your way, never forget that God is still in control of your life and that He has a plan for you.

How do you imagine Manoah's wife felt when she finally saw her dream coming true? _____

_____

_____

_____

What dream are you waiting to have answered? _____

_____

_____

_____

2. She held on to the truth, even when her husband was afraid and doubted. (See Judg. 13:22,23.)

The truth of God's love for you is written in His Word. You need to read it, study it, meditate on it, and memorize it. Hide God's Word in your heart, and allow it to calm your fears and settle your doubts. Samson's mother believed what the angel had said and used the truth of God's words to quell her fear.

If you aren't reading the Word of God, watch out! You are leaving yourself open for disappointment, fear, and doubt to pounce on you and choke out your relationship with God. Remember to follow Samson's mother's example and hang on to the truth in God's Word when your emotions want to get the best of you.

Are you reading the Bible on a regular basis? Yes_____ No_____

If you answered no, set a time and place each day that you can begin spending time in God's Word.

Time: _____ Place: _____

3. She never quit praying and believing the best for Samson. (See Judg. 16:31.)

Samson brought great disappointment to his mother most of his adult life, and yet she still loved and accepted him. I believe that it was the prayers of his mother that led to the eventual change of

Samson's rebellious heart. After he lost his life taking vengeance on the Philistines, his mother accepted him and brought him home to a place of burial and rest with the family.

It is important to note that while Samson often disappointed his mother, God never disappointed her. Be careful that you don't blame God for how people act. People will sometimes disappoint us, but God never will. He is faithful. While you face disappointments, never quit talking to God in prayer about your feelings and have faith to believe that God is still in control, because He always is. God is faithful even when we aren't. We can trust Him completely.

Read 2 Timothy 2:11-13. Write out verse 13: _____

_____

118

Remember that Jesus never quits praying and believing the best for you. He sits at the right hand of Father God and pleads your case every day. He reminds Him to see your sin through the blood that He shed on the cross. He bore our transgressions (our sin) on that cross, taking the punishment we deserve. (See 2 Cor. 5;21.)

Reflections

Now take a look into your own heart. You were asked earlier to identify what you have been carrying in your "suitcase." On the lines below, ask Jesus, the great Intercessor, to help you to give up any pain, frustration, or disappointment that you may have been dragging around. _____

_____

_____

Remember to follow the example of Samson's mother, Manoah's wife: Never give up your hope and faith in God, hold on to the truth, even when others doubt, and never quit praying and believing for God's best for your life.

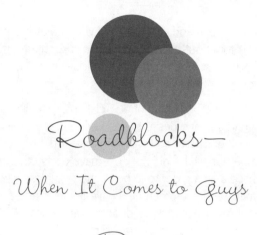

Roadblocks—

When It Comes to Guys

Part 1

Unhealthy/Ungodly Relationships

by Suzanne Rentz

I was setting up the chairs while I heard them talking. The Bible study was about to start, and they said, "He's traveled with 'Athletes in Action,' and he's in the paper all the time giving God the glory for his football success. I think it's going to be good tonight." *Who could that be? I thought. I know everyone in my small town; I don't know of any Christian athletes who went on a trip like this.*

As we all sat down, I glanced up to see who had entered the room. Suddenly my heart was pounding as my eyes met his. He was absolutely gorgeous, "Eyes of blue, six foot two." It was hard to concentrate on what he was saying. I actually don't remember a word; I was too busy calculating. Okay, he's gorgeous, a Christian, athletic, nice build, went on a missions trip, speaks in youth groups—what else was there? He was the man I'd been waiting for, the man of my dreams.

We started out as friends. He seemed very moral. We hung out (sort of dated) for about three months. It was soon after that when we kissed for the first time; then it was official—we were boyfriend and girlfriend.

I remember in the beginning of our relationship feeling a little unsatisfied. I had a strong desire to be cherished and fussed over. He had every other quality, so I was sure that would come in time. And, well, to be honest, he did not quite have every other quality. He did not have a strong desire to be in church, unless it was a Sunday morning, and even then he'd have a hard time paying attention. He'd hold my hand, whisper, doodle, make jokes. He'd listen sometimes, but most of the time he wasn't soaking anything in.

One time while I was at his house I remember asking him where he was with the Lord. He got out a newspaper article written about himself and said, "This right here shows you—see how I think about God."

I began to realize that this relationship was not paradise. I saw things in him that were not quite right. But there was a reason that justified it. You see, his parents had hurt him when he was young. They seemed to love to encourage him only in his athletics. They took him to church, but they had a horrible marriage and divorced. Soon I became convinced that I was the one who could make the difference in his life. If I could love him enough, believe in him enough, I knew he'd change.

While I was on my "change crusade," we started getting more involved physically. Our kisses were no longer just kisses. Slowly I was compromising. I was not only innocent, but naïve. It seemed he just kept pushing the whole physical thing more and more. He wasn't ever satisfied.

I had always dreamed of being in a relationship, but I had never determined what boundaries or standards I should stick to. I also was not accountable to anyone. Instead, I had this blind trust in him.

Although our relationship continued, we both moved in different directions. We'd see each other often; we wrote and sent letters.

The desire kept our relationship exciting, and the physical part just kept getting worse. The Holy Spirit convicted us, but we just ignored Him. I kept hoping for change, and yet instead of his becoming a better person, I was becoming less and less of who I wanted to be. Being a Christian and serving God were not easy because my heart was becoming more and more calloused. The "shame factor" entered in. I knew what was right, and yet I wasn't doing it.

Soon it became easier to work or do something else on Sundays so I wouldn't have to confront the truth. The more I stayed away the less committed I felt. I put my emphasis on being successful, on a career that would make me feel good about myself.

We broke up many times, we were even "engaged" once, and yet I couldn't get out. I felt as though I might as well stop trying; it was as if I was forever connected to him. Besides, I could never love any man the way I loved him. He had my heart!

So there I was, successful in my career, distant from church, and in a bad relationship. Then one day I made a decision. I wanted my life to count. I was numb on the inside, and I wanted to feel again. I missed my relationship with Jesus and godly Christian friends. The friends I was presently hanging around with were so superficial. I lost sight of the dreams I had had as a young girl. There was only one way out—I had to start making different choices.

I made a commitment to myself to start going to church again, at least for thirty days. I was going to go every opportunity that came up. The first few times I went were tough. No one reached out or befriended me. The services seemed so long and boring. But I had made a commitment. I knew I had to stick it out for the full thirty days, so whether I felt like going or not, I continued. Soon someone did reach out to me, and it made going to church much easier. Before long, at one of the services, the Lord spoke to me; I actually felt a burning sensation inside, and a nervousness, almost a butterflies-in-the-stomach kind of feeling, during the service. I responded at the altar. I was finally right with the Lord in church, but that was only half the battle. The other half was breaking off the relationship that had me in bondage.

It was raining that night, and we were sitting in the parking lot. I told him that this time the breakup was for good. He cried and pleaded with me, making heart-wrenching remarks like, "I thought you loved me. You can't do this!" But I sat there with my face set like flint, unmoved. I told him he had to break every tie. The conversation lasted about an hour. As I drove away, I felt like someone had taken a knife and stabbed me in the heart. I felt sick in my head and in my heart. My world had crumbled. What I had given—heart, mind, and soul—had failed. I was raw inside, and I sat with my hands on the wheel, crying, "God, get me through this!"

The story doesn't end there. It wasn't that easy; he made a few attempts to get back together. Some days I couldn't stop thinking about him and the good times we had shared. My heart still felt "in love" with him, and at times, doing what was right seemed confusing. My emotions and feelings were often so overwhelming that I had to remind myself, "I will get through this fog." I'd tell God, "I will be obedient—You know what's best for me."

There were many heart-to-heart talks with God. And I often meditated on (thought about) Psalm 130, which talks about God's forgiveness, about hoping in the Lord, and about restoration. I came to a new, intimate place with God. I had waffled so much in the past that I knew I was too vulnerable to see him, even as a "friend," so I stuck to my guns.

As time went on, the pain lessened. I took some great classes called "Reconcilers" (reconciling yourself to God, and then yourself) at my church. I also went to see a Christian counselor. I wanted to be healthy, emotionally and spiritually. I continued to attend church, to pray, and to read the Bible, and I fellowshipped with Christian friends.

Let me add one more thing to this story. I mentioned that I thought I'd never feel the same way towards another man. That was a lie that the devil tried to use to trap me. Later, I did meet my

Prince Charming. He was handsome, godly, and had a great personality. But what I was most attracted to was his heart after God. And he was so romantic! I have such a wonderful marriage. I still admire my husband, and we have been married for eight years, have three beautiful sons, and are in ministry together.

God has so richly blessed my life. As I look back, I see that I made some hard decisions, but God took my hand and helped me get through them. All things are possible with God by your side. When you stop believing in yourself, God still believes in you!

Reflections

After Suzanne began dating her "dream man," she began to see that he wasn't everything she thought he was. What did she do? What should she have done? What would you have done?

_____

_____

_____

Suzanne found herself caught in an unhealthy relationship because she had failed to plan ahead. She wrote, "I had failed to determine what boundaries and standards I would stick to." When you fail to plan, you plan to fail. Take time now to determine what your boundaries will be in a dating relationship. Measure your standards to God's Word. How do they line up?

_____

_____

_____

Another area that Suzanne failed to determine was in the area of accountability. In other words, nobody knew what she was or

*wasn't doing. Whom do you trust and feel comfortable to share
your standards with?* _____

_____

_____

_____

124

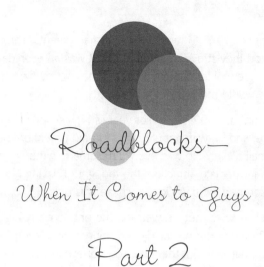

Roadblocks—
When It Comes to Guys

Part 2

Sex and Pregnancy
Before Marriage

by Sarah King

Today as I looked out the window, I watched my husband as he tied the string to our son's kite. Ryan looked at his daddy, anticipating the moment his toy would be in the air. The five-year-old ran as fast as he could until the wind pulled the kite into the sky. As soon as it went up, the kite came falling down. At the same moment, I suddenly heard a loud *crash* in the house.

The noise startled me. I walked into the next room to find Isaac under a bucket of toys. I laughed at the one-year-old as he peeked up from under the brim of the bucket. As I bent down to scoop him up, his big blue eyes looked into mine. Those eyes reminded me of a pair that looked at me four years ago, a time when my life was empty.

I was born in 1975 to two loving, Christian parents. Throughout my childhood they strove to see that Christ was an everyday part of my life. As I grew older, though, I started making my own choices. One choice would make a lifelong impact.

I met "John" in 1992, my junior year of high school. He was tall, he was nice, and he was popular. Oh, and did I mention that he was a football player? He was every girl's dream. Although there was not an immediate attraction, the thought of having him as a boyfriend seemed exciting. So, the chase was on!

The first week we met we were on the phone every night for hours. We talked about his family and mine, past relationships, football—you name it. But there was one question still left unasked: Was he a Christian? Now, you might think I would have known by the way he talked to me or the words he used, but I didn't. He didn't swear. He was very calm and well-mannered. He was clean-cut. He sounds just like a Christian, right?

Well, the day finally came to find out. I had to work up the courage to ask, and I wasn't sure I wanted to hear his answer. I think deep down inside I knew what it would be. But I asked him anyway.

"Uh…um…are you a um…a Christian? Or…um…do you go to church?" The words fell out of my mouth, and I stumbled over every one of them.

"Well, I go to church sometimes and…." Once I heard the word *church* I tuned him out. I knew what the answer was. Yep, that's it! He was definitely the one for me! Little did I know how wrong I would be.

Seven months later and several attempts to try and get John to go to church with me, he finally accepted my invitation.

Oh boy! I thought. *This is it! He's going to go to the altar, repent, and get saved.*

Well, after no emotion, and after he sat there mocking the people speaking in tongues, I realized it would be harder than I thought.

126

You see, I was already committed to him. In the beginning I thought I could change him. And I did stay strong, for a while. Then little by little my guard went down. At first, it was kissing him and lying to my parents about where I had been and with whom I had been. Then it went to heavy kissing and petting and sneaking out of the house to meet him, and it went from there. He really didn't care *about* me and what I wanted out of the relationship. What he did care about was what he could get *from* me, and what he could get out of the relationship. So, instead of my changing him, he slowly and surely changed me.

After being in the relationship for about a year, I started to question my relationship with the Lord. I hardly ever prayed unless John and I were fighting or if I was asking God to "Please help me not be pregnant!" I remember driving home from his house one time and feeling as if the Lord were clearly showing me that if I continued in this relationship I would not make it to heaven. Sadly enough, that didn't matter to me. I was in love, and I wasn't going to let anyone break us up—not even God.

127

In the spring of 1994, I went back to school for an education in dental assisting. It would be a nine-month program, and although I didn't enjoy school, I figured it couldn't be too bad. After one month of school, I was getting pretty tired. I was having a hard time waking up in the morning, and I just wasn't feeling well. After two and a half months of feeling this way, and after missing my monthly cycle twice, I decided to finally take a pregnancy test.

I remember standing in the shower crying as the water rolled off my shoulders. I was talking to God and to my unborn baby, feeling hopeless, like a failure. I wanted so much to take back some of the things I had done, but it was too late.

I waited until I couldn't hide it any longer. When I told John, the first word out of his mouth was "abortion," but I couldn't and wouldn't do that.

I finished school, and one month later I gave birth to a baby boy. He had beautiful olive skin, dark curly hair, and big blue eyes. I wanted so much to raise this child in a family with a mommy and a daddy. I had seen so many times when a couple would split up, and the children were torn in two. It caused so much devastation. I wasn't going to let this happen to my "family."

The day John told me he had finally found a job was a happy one. I knew that he would now be the provider that I had always hoped for. After two weeks on the job, however, he came to my house and told me that he had quit. He told me it wasn't the job for him, and besides, he wasn't making enough money. He told me his friend was getting hired on somewhere else and promised he would check into it soon.

A month later and still jobless, John got kicked out of his parents' home. We went to my parents and begged for them to let him stay in their camper. He promised them that he would find a job and finally start providing for his child. On that condition, they decided he could stay.

After not seeing John for days at a time, my parents would come to me and ask where he had been. Being the trusting (and naive) person I was, I would always back him up, telling them that he was out looking for a job or that he was doing work for a friend. He would come back with new clothes and a haircut, sometimes smelling like alcohol. But I still insisted he was trying to provide for us and still trying to find a job.

Six months after John moved into the camper, he still had no job. Somehow he always found a reason to get money from me. He told me he would go to the store to pick up some of the things I needed for the baby. Hours later he would return home with nothing but a new tattoo or a bunch of drunken friends. He never bought anything for our son, not even a package of diapers. I was getting tired of the money being spent on worthless things. I was tired of the food being stolen out of my baby's mouth. But most of all, I was tired of the unkept promises.

Finally came the Sunday when I stepped into my home church for the first time in many months. I went because I wanted my son to be raised in church just as I had been. Although that should not have been my only reason, the Lord would use it to draw me back to Him.

That day I started thinking of the kind of influence and impact that John would have on this child's life. Would he grow up to serve the Lord if he was raised in a "family" like this? Would he respect women if he was raised to disrespect his own mother? How would he learn to be a good provider for his own family? What would his definition of "daddy" be? Well, I certainly didn't want it to be *Someone who runs around with other women; who only comes around to see me when he doesn't have a party to go to; who can't hold down a job; who can't keep a promise.* Those thoughts had a great effect on my life. So I decided to make some changes that would lead me down the road to where I am today.

God's desire was for me to follow *His* will for my life. I began to realize that by choosing *my* own will, I was digging myself into a deep hole. The only way for me to get out was to surrender my life to Him. After four years of Satan's lies, I realized that God wanted more for me. I ended the relationship with John not reluctantly, but excited for what the Lord had in store for me. I then rededicated my life to Him.

129

On April 27, 1997, I made a pledge for purity. On this night I received a ring and signed a pledge to God and to my future husband to remain pure until I was married. I wept during the ceremony, remembering my past. I wept because of God's mercy on me. I wept because regardless of what had happened, I was forgiven.

In the winter of 1997, I married Brandon King, a handsome, caring, godly man. When the Lord united us as one, He also united a family. Brandon is Ryan's provider, nurturer, disciplinarian, encourager, and friend. Brandon is also Ryan's daddy, and you would never guess any different. We hope that one day soon Brandon will be allowed to adopt Ryan. All the fears I ever had of raising Ryan in a home torn in two are now just memories.

As I look back, I can see all that the Lord has brought me through. He has taken me to greater places than I could ever have imagined, places I could not have reached on my own. He can do the same for you. All you have to do is surrender your life to Him, and He will take care of the rest.

"For I know the plans I have for you," declares the Lord, plans to prosper you and not to harm you, plans to give you hope and a future."
Jeremiah 29:11

Reflections

Sarah allowed herself to become emotionally committed to "John" before she even knew if he was a Christian. Write out 2 Corinthians 6:14: _____

130

_____

_____

Do you think it is wise for a Christian to date a non-Christian? Why or why not? _____

_____

_____

"Instead of my changing him, he was slowly and surely changing me." Sarah's statement was profound. Even as she realized that "John" was turning her into someone she didn't want to be, she turned her back on God and stayed in the relationship, never stopping to think about the pain and destruction she would have to face. Do you ever find yourself doing, saying, and becoming exactly what you don't want to? Who are you living your life to please? God? Your boyfriend? Your friends? What happens when we try to please others instead of God?

_____

_____

Sarah found herself getting way too physically involved with "John." How did this happen? How could she have avoided this pitfall?

Romans 8:28 says that God works all things together for good for "those who love him, who have been called according to his purpose." God miraculously turned Sarah's "tragedy" into a "trophy" by putting her life back together. What did Sarah do to pave the way for God to repair her heart and life?

131

Some young women might say, "Everything worked out for Sarah. If I date a non-Christian, have sex before marriage, or even get pregnant, everything will work out for me in the end, too." For every testimony that has a happy ending, there are countless others that end in pain, sorrow, and utter disaster. Read Romans chapter 6. What is it saying about how we choose to live our lives?

Roadblocks—
When It Comes to Guys

Part 3

Abortion

by Yolanda Benjamin

Please be advised: *Because of society's lack of honesty in dealing with abortion, I felt it was necessary to shed light on the reality of abortion. Abortion is the taking of human life. While I have not described in detail how the actual horrible procedure is done, I do discuss my feelings before and after and the terrible effect abortion had on my life.*

Romans 6:23 tells us, "For the wages of sin is death, but the gift of God is eternal life in Christ Jesus our Lord." Growing up as a preacher's kid, I wish I would have believed that verse! I might have never taken "life" into my own hands.

I was engaged to be married at the age of 18 and already had lost my virginity. We went to a key leader of the church and told him we were going to postpone our wedding because I was pregnant. His advice to us was to get an abortion since it would save my father's reputation. The number one reason for abortion is to save a relationship, or so we were told.

I made the doctor's appointment to have the abortion. I was so young, and I don't remember the ordeal itself. When I woke up from the abortion procedure, I felt a void but buried it deep inside of me and never spoke of it. I was very sick when I arrived home; I climbed into bed feeling weak and nauseated, and I slept. It was at this point my heart became hard, causing me to make bad choices time and time again, choices that I will always regret.

The only people who knew, other than the doctor, were my mother and my fiancé. We went ahead and married in the church as if nothing had happened.

Four years and two babies later, I found myself pregnant again. This time we were financially strapped. The only thing in our food pantry was a can of formula. How were we going to support another baby? The only solution we knew of was to have another abortion. Since a "leader in the church" (speaking out of ignorance) had approved the first one, we didn't see a problem with this one. What we failed to realize is what Psalm 139 teaches: that even in a mother's womb, a unique person is being shaped by God for a special role in God's plan. (See vv. 13,15,16.)

There's no doubt—God is pro-life. I should have never acted on man's opinion; instead, I should have stood on God's Word. John 10:10 says, "The thief comes only to steal and kill and destroy; I have come that they [that means you] may have life, and have it to the full [or more abundantly]." Sin numbs you to the truth.

This time the appointment was made in an abortion clinic. The only thing I remember was an eerie death and cold feeling when I entered the building. I was given a pill to relax, and then only dead silence was around me. I could feel the pain of the other women who were there for the same reason, but we couldn't look each other in the eye.

This abortion only added death to my spirit and my livelihood. It also led to the destruction of my marriage and brought a godless

133

man into my life in an adulterous affair. Death had entered my very being. The affair with this man even brought another abortion appointment. I didn't want to be tied down.

I believe I used a false name for my third abortion because of my shame. This time I felt the excruciating pain, and I remember most of the procedure. I will spare you all the awful details of how it is done, but finally I passed out. When it was over, I was awakened by the attending nurse and smelling salts, and I remember wishing I had died at that very moment. Believe me, when I walked out of the clinic, I was full of anger and hatred towards men and myself.

One of the results of abortion is often promiscuity. Actually, it can become a cycle—one leads right back to the other—because you keep making the same wrong choices. I continued to search for love in the wrong places.

Then I met Darwin, who later became my husband. He was charming and everything I had ever wanted in a man. To my surprise, I was challenged in every way, but especially to remain his number one girl, not number three. I thought I could trap him by becoming pregnant. Drugs and alcohol had the best of me. I was addicted; I was trying to cover up my deep pain.

When I announced to him that I was pregnant, my world was rocked. He said with no uncertainty that he wasn't going to be trapped like that. He told me to get an abortion, and I agreed. I would have done whatever it took to keep him.

On our way to the clinic, I cried uncontrollably from my inner-most being. I knew the emotional and physical pain I was going to face. I asked for two Valiums instead of one. I daydreamed that Darwin would come into the clinic and tell me he would marry me, and we would sail off into the sunset. He did come, but he said he would continue doing his own thing, and I could keep the baby. Instead, pride got in the way, and I proceeded into the room and waited for my sentencing—"death."

That cold, dreadful place was haunting me with every step I took towards the condemned room. I was a prisoner of my own decision. I felt as if I were walking in slow motion—a dead woman walking around with numbness and no emotions. I was full of anxiety, hopelessness, and a sense of being lost. I hated getting on that bed; I knew what was coming. Desperation and guilt set in.

By now, my mind was racing, thinking how I could turn around and run out of that clinic. I wanted everything to come to a halt. I wanted to yell, "*Stop!* I've changed my mind!" While the tears were still running down my face, the medication hit me, and I was fast asleep. Darkness was around me once more, and I didn't care if I ever woke up again.

I grew up in church, yet I failed to follow Christ. My rebellion against God caused me to do things I never thought I was capable of doing. I've experienced trauma, but I thank God that He has healed me—physically, emotionally, and spiritually. It took me twenty years and God's help to face what I had done. God made a way to bring dignity, honor, and respect to the babies I killed.

My husband, Darwin, committed his life to Christ; then a month later everything changed dramatically when I rededicated my life to God. Now years later, we are partners in ministry together.

These wounds have been healed by way of having a proper memorial for those precious babies. Our ministry, Truth Ministries (The Road Unto Thy Healing), offers God's forgiveness to others who have had abortions and to ourselves as well. He restores us and brings reconciliation to the babies and parents in the spirit of our Lord.

Many women and men feel we've been forgiven, but what we fail to realize is that we may not have been healed emotionally. For example, have we grieved and connected our emotions towards the abortions? This is why in our ministry we hold a one-day, intense "Memorial Session" for men and women who have gone through an abortion. Because of my own devastating abortion experience, I believe it's vital to attend this kind of session on behalf of these babies. During these sessions, God allows the hidden area of abortion to be exposed. He creates an atmosphere where we who have been hurt feel safe and comforted by the Holy Spirit.

Now I can say I am a proud mother of ten: four living children, four aborted, one miscarriage, and Natasha, who died at five days old. My aborted babies—Daniel, Sheila, Christina, Jonathan (miscarried), and Marcus—are being held in the loving arms of Jesus, and I wait excitedly to be reunited with them in heaven one day. God alone can comfort the haunting memories and bring mourning to joy.

Reflections

Four inconvenient pregnancies—four innocent babies murdered. Yolanda's promiscuity resulted in pregnancies neither she nor the men she slept with were ready for. What need in her life drove her into these physical relationships?

_____

_____

Yolanda received a lot of bad advice. Against what should we judge all counsel? What should we consult before we make any major decisions?

_____

In today's society many people believe that it is "a woman's right to choose" whether or not she will go through with an unwanted pregnancy. Do you believe that this is true? What does God's Word say about this? Is it a woman's right to choose if she will commit murder? Is abortion any different? What do you think?

_____

_____

_____

Yolanda said that many people experience God's forgiveness, but they have yet to have their "hearts healed." Can you relate to Yolanda's story? Do you need to experience the forgiveness and healing that only Jesus can bring? Surrender your whole heart to Him now. Let yourself face the pain of your past, and let the Holy Spirit breathe into your heart the joy that your future will bring. Surrender; be healed, in Jesus' name.

137

Roadblocks—
When It Comes to Guys
Part 4

Abusive Relationships—
Verbal and Physical

by Lisa Spears

I was fifteen years old when he hit me the first time. Little did I know that the bruise I received from his fist would be the first of many. Over the next four and a half years of my teenage life, I would live in this silent prison of a relationship with someone who told me he loved me but who made my body a living punching bag. Of course, he would justify the cuts and bruises by blaming me for making him do it. If I accidentally made eye contact with another guy or if I returned from the store five minutes later than he expected, a fight would start and bruises would result. His unpredictable anger left me feeling continually afraid and uncertain of the next time he might get mad and hit me.

What hurt me worse than the physical abuse was what he said. He told me that I was nothing, that I would never amount to anything, and that no one else would ever want me. He told me that I provoked him to anger and that it was my fault he hit me, because I was so stupid. He told me that if I ever left him, he would make me regret it…and I believed him. My hopes of marrying the man of my dreams and of living a fairy-tale life were shattered more each day I stayed with him.

It was not long before I lost all my friends and became almost completely dependent on this man who sought to control my life. While I spent Friday nights sitting home alone, he would be out with other girls. Many nights I would cry myself to sleep, just to be awakened by the telephone and the laughter of other girls in the background as he fed me lie after lie about where he would be.

Knowing that he was seeing other girls caused me to become insecure and to fear that he might leave. I started believing that I needed to do more to make him happy so that he would stay with me. That's when I decided to give him the one thing that I had held on to so tightly all my life. I surrendered my purity and held out my whole heart, mind, and body for him to continue to abuse and destroy.

For four and a half years, I lived my life in continual fear, hurt, and hopelessness. I learned to bottle the anguish and loneliness deep inside. No matter how hard I tried to hide the abuse I was experiencing, the marks on my body gave evidence of the truth. There seemed to be no way out of this prison of a relationship. Eventually, though, because of the prayers and encouragement from family and friends, I gained the courage to leave the abuse.

It took me two years and a lot of tears to deal with the hurt I had hidden deep inside. My hopes and dreams for the future had been shattered, and I had no idea how to begin living again. I tried partying and drinking to numb the pain in my heart. I hung out with people who I thought were friends, but I found out that when

I was really in need and when I hit rock bottom in my life, they were nowhere around.

Rock bottom took the form of a deep-rooted depression. My mind had been so warped by the lies my boyfriend had told me that I truly believed no one would ever love me. Because I had given him my purity, I felt as though no other man would ever want me. My every hope and dream had been completely shattered, and my heart had been torn to pieces. That's when I turned to God to get me out of the mess my life had become.

You see, I had been brought up in church. I knew how to "walk the walk" and "talk the talk," but I had never really depended on God to lead me in the right direction. I had always thought that I had a pretty good handle on my own life. I did not need God's help; I was fine on my own. But looking back at the abuse from which I had narrowly escaped, I decided that controlling my own life had almost killed me inside and out.

So I started going back to church and began meeting with one of the pastors for counseling every week. With his help and with the countless hours of prayer and encouragement from friends and family, I began allowing the Lord to gently pick up the broken pieces of my heart and put them back together again. The hurt, disappointment, and hopelessness were soon replaced by a will to fight for my life.

I began memorizing Scriptures like Romans 8:37 that says, "…we are more than conquerors through Him who loved us," and Philippians 4:13 that says, "I can do all things through him [Christ] who gives me strength." A woman in my church who didn't know anything about what I was going through gave me Isaiah 41:10 NKJV which says, "Fear not, for I am with you; be not dismayed, for I am your God. I will strengthen you, yes, I will help you, I will uphold you with My righteous right hand." I began to live my life by this Scripture, and it helped me through some of the painful and lonely times.

Since then, I have grown to truly understand my need for God. He has allowed me to learn about and experience forgiveness, hope, and joy, and has taught me to begin dreaming again. I am going to a Christian college to earn my master's degree in marriage and family therapy. The best part of my story is that I have met and married the man of my dreams, the one with whom God has destined me to share my life. Through working in youth ministry together, my husband and I have a desire to bring hope and a future to those who have lost their ability to dream by sharing our lives with them.

Reflections

"My hopes of marrying the man of my dreams and living a fairy-tale life were shattered more each day that I stayed with him," Lisa wrote. Why in the world did she continue to date him?

141

_____

_____

_____

Do you know anyone who is in an abusive relationship? Are you in a relationship with someone who hurts you verbally, emotionally, or physically? If so, get out of it before it is too late!

_____

_____

_____

After four and a half years of pain and abuse, Lisa managed to escape. What finally helped her to leave the relationship? "The _____ and _____ from friends and family."

Even after escaping the abusive relationship, Lisa continued down a road of self-destruction. What was the real root of her problems?_____

_____

_____

What is the thing that motivated her to stay in an abusive relationship and to make such horrible choices for her life after the relationship ended? _____

_____

_____

What was her need?_____

_____

_____

What is your greatest need? How are you seeking to have that need met? _____

_____

_____

Pick out the one Scripture from Lisa's testimony that encouraged you the most. Write it out and explain why it encouraged you.

_____

_____

_____

Someday My Prince Will Come

by Erin E. Zonio

Do you remember watching the movie *Cinderella* as a little girl and dreaming of your Prince Charming? Tall, dark, and handsome, he sweeps you off your feet, and as Cinderella did, you live happily ever after. Every good fairy tale ends in eternal bliss.

But when will *my* "happily ever after" come? Almost every little girl has heard those dream-inspiring words over and over again. Yet one day, most of us wake up from those dreams and realize that real life doesn't consist of balls, carriages, and princes. Rather, it sometimes seems full of mean stepmothers, wicked step-sisters, and a house that always needs more cleaning. Life can be hard; dreams can sometimes seem as if they will never come true.

Maybe your dreams don't involve a Prince Charming; maybe your heart's desires are a little different. Yet still you feel they will *never* come true. You feel you won't ever be the person you want to be; you will never have what your heart longs for, and you ask, "Why not me?"

You can be assured that you are not the only person who has ever felt this way. And you can also be confident that God, our heavenly Father, the all-knowing Creator, knit you together in such a special way that He knows your deepest desires. Not only does He know your desires, but He is the one who gave them to you.

What are your heart's desires?

List a few of your most precious dreams:

I hope _____

I hope _____

I hope _____

I hope _____

Now ask yourself if these desires are pure. Do they please God? Are they honorable?

Read Psalm 139 (pay special attention to verse 23). Name some things about you that God knows:

_____

144

_____

_____

_____

Now read Jeremiah 29:11-14.

What does all this say about your heavenly Father, your Creator, regarding your dreams? _____

_____

_____

_____

_____

That's wonderful! So now what?

Surrender your dreams to your heavenly Father.

I've heard of a song about the Lord that says that nothing we desire compares with Him. That is how our attitude should be toward everything in life—our love for Jesus and our desire to serve Him should never be overshadowed by our love or desire for anything else—even *good* things.

Exodus 20:3-5 says, "You shall have no other gods before me [God]. You shall not make for yourself an idol in the form of anything...You shall not bow down to them or worship them; for I, the Lord your God, am a jealous God...." No, this is not implying that you throw away all your pictures of Brian (or Scott, or whatever his name may be)! But what is your ultimate desire?

All other desires need to be surrendered to the Lord. That means to give Him control of your life. Let your love for Him and desire to know Him become the top priority of every day of your life. Ask Him to bring you to the point where you can say, "All that matters now is Jesus," and He gently and lovingly will.

Read the following verses, and think about how each will encourage and help you surrender completely to Him:

145

Proverbs 3:5,6 _____

Ecclesiastes 3:11 _____

Romans 8:28 _____

James 1:17 _____

2 Timothy 1:12 _____

I encourage you to pray this daily: *God, bring me to the place where I know for certain that I can completely trust You.*

Seek the Lord with all of your heart. There is nothing more satisfying in life than a relationship with Jesus. You can have all your dreams come true, but if you don't know Jesus, you will not be satisfied. You see, not only did He create you with desires and the ability to dream, but He also created you with a hole, an emptiness, a void inside that can only be filled by Him. He wants a relationship with you, and He created you to want a relationship with Him. Sometimes, the hardest part is getting to know Him; it may seem easier to try to fill that void by doing our own thing, and by trying to fulfill *our* goals and dreams. But it will never work; the empty feeling will always be there. That's a fact.

So why not try seeking God with all of your heart as Jeremiah 29:13 says to do. You will be so glad that you did!

The following are some Scriptures that people like to read when they desire and want things, but only the first half of each verse has been printed. Before we examine some of the promises of God, let's look at some of the commands. Even though it may not be what we want to do, the command is just as important as the promise.

As you read the verses, think about what practical application each of these has in your life. What will you do to obey these commands?

"Delight yourself in the Lord..." (Ps. 37:4). To obey this I can

_____

_____

_____

"Commit your way to the Lord; trust in him..." (Ps. 37:5). To obey this I can _____

_____

_____

"But seek first His kingdom and His righteousness..." (Matt. 6:33). To obey this I can _____

_____

_____

You will begin to live when you lose yourself in God's purpose for you!

Now watch what God does!

146

When you come to a place of such fulfillment in your relationship with Jesus, that's when He can truly bless you. Seeing your dreams fulfilled will be the icing on the cake. Your life will be a blessing to others, and you will feel overwhelmed by all that God does in your life. Here are those Scriptures again, but this time with the promise, too, of what God's going to do when you surrender to Him and seek Him with all of your heart:

"Delight yourself in the Lord and he will give you the desires of your heart" (Ps. 37:4).

"Commit your way to the Lord; trust in him and he will do this: He will make your righteousness shine like the dawn…" (Ps. 37:5,6).

"But seek first his kingdom and his righteousness, and all these things will be given to you as well" (Matt. 6:33).

He fathoms the remotest abyss of my heart, and He satisfies it![1]   147

Most wonderful love

Most women long to give themselves completely to another—to have a deep "soul" relationship with the man of their dreams, to be loved thoroughly and exclusively by him. But I believe that the following message by an unknown author is a word from God to His daughters.

No, not until you are satisfied, fulfilled, and content with being loved by Me alone—with giving yourself totally and unreservedly to Me, to having an intensely personal and unique relationship [with Me] that I have planned for you. You will never be truly united with another until you are united with Me—exclusive of anyone or anything else, exclusive of any desires or longings.

I want you to stop planning, stop wishing, and allow Me to give you the most thrilling plan existing, one you cannot imagine. I want you to have the best. Please allow Me to bring it to you. You just keep watching Me, accepting the greatest things. Keep experiencing the satisfaction that I am. Keep listening and learning the things I

tell you [in your heart and in My Word], and just be willing to wait—
that's all.

Don't be anxious; don't worry; don't look around at the things
that you think you want. Just keep looking off and away up to Me
or you'll miss what I want to show you.

Then, when you're ready, I'll surprise you with a love far more
wonderful than any you would dream of or imagine possible. You
see, until you are ready and until the one I have for you is ready (I
am working even this moment to have both of you ready at the
same time), until you are both satisfied exclusively with Me and the
life that I have prepared for you, you won't be able to experience
the love that exemplifies your relationship with Me and is, thus,
perfect love.

And, Dear One, I want you to have this most wonderful love. I
want you to see, in the flesh, a picture of your relationship with Me
and to enjoy materially and concretely the everlasting union of
beauty, perfection, and love that I offer you with Myself. Know that I
love you utterly. Believe it, and be satisfied.

Unknown

148

Design Your Destiny

by Suzanne Rentz

I remember lying in bed one night when I was a little girl, trying to go to sleep. I counted sheep, I made shadows on the wall with my hands, but I still lay there, restless. I was finally growing tired when something stirred in my heart. I had a vision of myself speaking to a large group of women from a pulpit. As I told them how much God loved them, my eyes filled with tears. It was as if I could feel or sense God's love for them, and they couldn't grasp it. That was years ago, and that vision became a faded memory that I misplaced for a while.

As a young girl in junior and senior high school, I had so many insecurities. I loved God and wanted to please Him, but I struggled to be liked and accepted by others. My practical sister would often tell me, "Be yourself," but I didn't know who I was. I knew what I wasn't; I wasn't the prettiest, the best dressed, or the most popular, and I didn't have a wealthy family. The funny thing was that as I grew closer to God and read the Bible, I hungered to become a woman of God. At a young age, I decided that God could help me be myself.

I was nineteen when I decided to go away to Bible college for a year to build a spiritual foundation in my life. It was *wonderful.* I remember looking at the pastors' and evangelists' wives, wondering what it would be like to be one of them, and what it would be like to be in ministry. It seemed like a dream I would never reach, and I often struggled to understand what it meant to be "called" into ministry.

I would have stayed at the Bible college longer, but I didn't know if God had *called* me to be in ministry. I had never been zapped by lightning or seen a burning bush or had a prophetic word given to me—but I definitely had the *desire* to be in ministry.

In my early twenties, I pursued a career in real estate, and I was determined to be successful. Selling, marketing, and climbing the corporate ladder were my goals, although when I met people who had "made it" in that business, I could see that for many of them their personal and family lives were unraveling. Their families were lost, and their unhappiness was evident; work had become their god. I knew this wasn't what I wanted. This was not my dream.

One Sunday I drove to see my old youth pastor, and I was reminded of my high school days. Back then I was so on fire for the Lord. Just being around him (my youth pastor) was such an encouragement. I realized the direction I was heading no longer appealed to me. On the way home, I determined to make some changes in my life. I wanted my life to count, and I didn't want to grow old with regrets; I wanted to make a difference, even while I was young. Within a week I started meeting with some girls at my church and leading a Bible study. Sometimes our Bible study would have more than twenty young women in attendance. Needing a name for our group, we decided to call it Daughters of Heaven.

Recently, I found a letter that I had written to a friend a while ago. In the letter I had said these words: "I don't know why, but I really have this desire to train young women to become women of God. I love the Bible studies I've been doing. I wonder if God could use me in this area?"

Looking back, I can see that God had taken my hand while I was a little girl and had directed my steps—then and now. He is still at work designing my destiny.

Did you know that God has a destiny for your life? The devil wants to stop that from happening, but he can't unless you allow him to because he's a defeated foe (Jesus defeated him on the cross 2,000 years ago).

Read John 10:10. The devil has come to steal, kill, and destroy God's very best for your life. One way he tries to do that is through insecurities.

Have you ever felt that you are not good enough? If the devil can convince you of that, then you are no threat to him. The sad thing is that the devil can discourage you through your family, your friends, your peers. The world portrays success, fame, and popularity as "arriving." The world's standards say that if you don't have those things, then you are "less than" or "not as good as" those who do.

God's standards are very different from the world's. Unfortunately, sometimes the world's standards creep into the church. We elevate those who are talented and gifted, even the evangelists, and we put them on pedestals; we compare ourselves with them. That breaks God's heart, because He wants you to be you. And although God calls us and speaks to us in different ways, one way is not better than another. God has had His hand in our lives; sometimes we just need to look.

151

Look at your life. Has God spared you or saved you from disaster? Has He given you a desire or a dream that you have forgotten? Have you had an awesome experience with God your Father when He spoke to you in your heart or in His Word? Take a few minutes to pray and search your heart.

Write down the times in your life that stand out. _____

_____

_____

_____

_____

An important thing that you should keep in mind is that God has called all of us to fulfill His specific plan for our lives. He is "...no respecter of persons" (Acts 10:34.) You can find out what God has called you to do by asking Him and developing your relationship with Him through reading His Word and talking to Him daily.

When the devil tries to discourage us by saying we are not "good enough," we must remind him of a few Scripture verses that tell what God says about us.

Write out and memorize these verses:

Philippians 4:13 _____

_____

_____

_____

Jeremiah 29:11 _____

_____

_____

_____

Ephesians 6:10-18 _____

_____

_____

_____

_____

Yes, the devil can use our feelings of insecurity to rob us of God's best, but another major weapon he'll use is *bitterness.*

The best way to describe bitterness is to think of an ugly, creepy tick. You might wonder what a tick and unforgiveness have in common, so let's compare.

You don't know when a tick latches onto you. It's very sneaky, often hidden in a spot that you don't see. It starts getting at you on the surface of your skin, and then goes deeper. It grows as it sucks your blood. Soon it has a hold on you, and you can't remove it except by completely destroying it with a match. Once you kill it, it must be removed before the wound will heal. If not removed, this small, insignificant bug can cause great damage: a high fever and infection in your whole body.

Unforgiveness is the true disease that causes bitterness. We don't always know that there is bitterness in our heart. It starts out with a numb feeling, maybe an "I don't care" attitude. Maybe someone hurts us, and instead of letting go, the hurt stays in our heart and grows. That's why we must be on guard.

Many Christians have talent, but some of them have never used it. In some cases God could have used them mightily, but they never dealt with their unforgiveness. Like a crippling disease, it has taken over their lives. They have missed God's very best, and instead of making their lives count, those talents and gifts lie buried, wasted. Those people are restless and searching; unless they allow God to destroy the "tick" of unforgiveness and bitterness, it will stay buried, causing more and more damage. We can't get rid of the "tick"; only God can.

153

Reflections

Examine your heart. Is it pure, or are there any traces of bitterness and unforgiveness? Have you been hurt recently by someone, or have you been holding on to something for years? Explain.

Read Psalm 139:1-18.

Always remember that God created you, and He loves you. From the moment you were conceived, when you were a little girl, and even now, your heavenly Father is at work designing your destiny.

Happily Ever After

by Shereen Christian

I am growing more in love with my "Prince" every day. (Isa. 9:6.) My life is not perfect, but as I go through it, I go with Him by my side. When I have troubles, I have a peace, knowing that I don't go through them alone. He is always there for me. Each day I make choices, and sometimes sacrifices, but I know that my life has meaning and purpose.

In Jeremiah 29:11 CEV, God talks about the plans He has for me.

> I will bless you with a future filled with hope—a future of success, not of suffering.

God's plan for my life is so much better than any fairy tale. It is so much more exciting, abundant, and rewarding than I could have ever wished or planned for myself. God has taken the things in my life that I thought could never be of any use and has turned them into something wonderful—a way to minister to the hearts of others. He has taken my "ashes" and turned them into beauty. (See Isa. 61:3.) Where there was deadness in my heart, He breathed new life. Where there were thorns and briars, He planted a beautiful garden.

God has truly blessed me in so many ways. Best of all, I can walk daily in His Presence, I can trust in His goodness, and I can rest assured, knowing that He loves me with an unconditional, everlasting love.

Day by day, my story goes on. New chapters will be written as my life unfolds. The exciting thing is that this story will never end! God is my real Prince, and I can truly live with Him in "His Kingdom" happily ever after—and so can you!

Reflections

I believe that God is speaking to His daughters through this wonderful excerpt from "He's Looking for a Bride" by Paige Chavoustie. I encourage you to read it as if it is a personal word from God to you!

"He did it for love. It was His love for you that brought Him to a manger as a Babe. It was His love for you that hung Him on a cross to take your sins and your shame onto His own body. It is His love for you that cleanses you with fuller's soap and the washing of the water by the Word of God. It is His love for you that burns off the dross in the Refiner's fire. It is His love for you that keeps seeking you out in the night, bringing you back to His side. It is His love for you that wants you to be pure and holy and spotless so that when that Day comes, you will be a Bride fit for the King of glory. His arms are open wide. Will you come?"[1]

Created for Such a Time As This

Choices of
the Heart

Part 1

by Jennifer Davis

Having my hair cut is a major production. My hair stylist, Karen, always allows extra time for my appointment. She has learned that when it comes to my hair, it is difficult for me to make a choice.

Several years ago I had decided it was time for a change. Many people discouraged me, saying, "You have such pretty long hair." Pretty or not, I wanted a change. After asking at least twenty-five people what I should do, I headed for the stylist's salon.

It took forty-five minutes for Karen and me to agree upon what would take place. About an hour later, half of my hair lay in a pile on the floor, and I loved my new "shag." I had made a wise choice.

You and I probably make a million choices every day—what to eat, what to drink, where to eat, where to shop—we are always making choices. *Choice* can be defined as "...the act of choosing...the power of choosing...care in selecting...."[1]

Think of all the choices you have to make each day when you get ready to go to school. If you are anything like I was when *I* was in school, you start early in the morning to make sure everything is just right. You probably make choices about your...

Clothes   (Pants? Skirt? T-shirt? Sweater? Warm coat? Flannel?)

Shoes   (Dr. Martens? Vans? Nikes? Platforms?)

Hairstyle   (Up? Down? Barrettes? Headband? Scrunchi?)

Breakfast   (Pop-tarts? Bagels? Muffins? Cereal? McDonald's?)

Lunch   (Packed lunch? No lunch? Snack Shack @ school?)

Make-up   (Natural? Retro? Gothic?)

Jewelry   (Silver? Beaded? Gold? Trendy costume stuff?)

Choices are a part of our everyday lives. Each choice we make shapes who we are, what we are doing with our lives, whom we are doing it with, and how it will be done.

With each choice you have the power to determine the quality of your life and relationships. Throughout your junior high, senior high, and college years you will make some of the most important choices of your life. While your teen years may seem relatively short in relation to the rest of your life, the choices you make during these years will have a profound effect on what your adult life is like.

Each right or wrong choice you make helps shape your character (who you really are). Every friendship or relationship you choose and every activity you get involved with will help shape who you are. If you choose to make the same bad choices that your friends or even your parents have made, you will become like them. If you make the good choices you know that Jesus would make, you will be changed to be like Him. The choice is yours. I pray that you will choose wisely and that this devotional will help you in the choices you make.

Describe a time when you know you made the right choice in a tough situation. _____

_____

_____

160

Describe a time when you made the wrong choice.

_____

_____

_____

How did you feel?

_____

_____

_____

Choice started with our heavenly Father. Write out the following Scriptures to discover more about how you were chosen.

John 15:16 _____

_____

_____

Ephesians 1:4 _____

_____

_____

2 Thessalonians 2:13 _____

_____

_____

It is awesome to think that God chose us. As you have learned in the previous entries of this devotional, God created you with a plan and purpose in mind. As you learn to choose wisely, you will see that plan unfold.

Choice Equals Power

The power to choose was given to us by our heavenly Father. Desiring to have us *choose* to love and serve Him, rather than *programming* us to do so, He knit in us the ability to make our own choices. He has given us the freedom to make good choices and bad choices, the power to choose to love Him or to reject Him. The choice is ours.

The center of all our choices must be our desire and passion to have a greater heart of intimacy with God, to know Him so well and to be drawn so close that we think, act, sound, and look like Him. As we stay close to Him, we will make choices that please Him.

Your first and most important choice is one that Joshua in the Old Testament challenged the Israelites to make. Today and every day, this is your choice, too.

Choice #1: Choose to serve God.

Read Joshua 24. Joshua led the Israelites into the Promised Land. In chapter 24 Joshua gathered all the tribes and the elders, leaders, judges, and officials of Israel. He wanted to do the following:

Remind them of their history.

Recall God's faithfulness.

Renew their covenant with God.

After sharing with them, he asked them to make a choice.

Re-read Joshua 24:14-15. What choice did Joshua ask them to make? _____

_____

Re-write these verses in your own words as if God wrote them to teenagers today. _____

_____

162

In Joshua 24:16 the people responded to Joshua, saying, "We would never turn away from God! We choose to serve God!" Verses 24-25 say that the people promised to serve God and obey Him, so, "On that day Joshua made a covenant for the people...."

In order for the Israelites to choose to serve God, they had to "walk the talk." Just making a verbal commitment wasn't enough. It never is. They had to act on their commitment and throw away the idols they had been worshipping.

An idol is something or someone that you treat as more important than God. Many young women may choose to serve God while praying at a church altar but will never succeed because they don't act on their commitment. Rather than focusing on God and removing the idols from their lives, they allow things and people to keep them from fully choosing God. Clothes, popularity, relationships, drugs, and alcohol are just a few idols that many young women "serve." They may really want to serve God but feel trapped. The idols in their lives seem too important to give up. As a result, they never choose God.

163

Reflections

Do you have any "idols" in your life that you need to "throw away" so that you will be free to choose God? If so, what are they?

_____

_____

_____

Knowing that God has chosen you and that He has a purpose and plan for your life, will you choose to serve Him? _____

_____

_____

Make a decision to choose to serve God. Make a covenant with Him, and write Him a short note telling Him that you are committed to serving Him.

_____

_____

_____

164

Choices of the Heart

Part 2

by Jennifer Davis

Let's look at two more choices you must make.

Choice #2: Choose to have an undivided heart.

It is said that the safest place to be is in the center of God's will. To remain in the center of His will we must choose to serve God with an undivided heart. To be undivided is to have no separation. When someone says to you, "I'm listening; you have my undivided attention," they mean, "I am going to totally, completely listen to you right now."

In 1 Corinthians 7, the apostle Paul told the Corinthians that he wanted them to "…live in a right way in undivided devotion to the Lord" (v. 35).

Look up Psalm 86:11 to see how King David prayed for an undivided heart. As a young woman in this generation, there are thousands of activities and opportunities grabbing for your attention every day. Your family, friends, boyfriends, sports, work, and even school can keep your heart divided. These things and people are not necessarily bad for you. Some may even help you grow in your relationship with God. You probably wouldn't call them "idols" either, but because of your time schedule, you may find that they can distract you from God. You may even discover that you often depend on them instead of depending on God. They divide your heart.

What areas of your life, if any, do you see dividing your heart?

_____

_____

_____

_____

Why do you feel that it is so easy to allow these things to divide your heart? How do they distract you from God?

166

_____

_____

_____

Because God has unique and special plans for your life, you must be determined to remain focused on Him so that His plans and your dreams will be realized. Don't allow the busy activities of your day or even the people you love the most to pull you away from God. Don't let your heart become divided. Make David's prayer your own. Ask for an undivided heart.

When I was seventeen I was "loving life." I was very involved at school serving as class president and cheering on the varsity cheerleading squad. I had many friends and generally felt good about life. People said I had a bright future. The only problem was, I didn't know Jesus. I was like a beautiful temple that was empty on the inside.

Then, one hot summer day, my friend's mother introduced me to Jesus Christ. I received Him into my heart instantly. After asking forgiveness for my sins, I promised to serve Him for the rest of my life—I *chose* to serve Him. I believe that heaven rejoiced. I left my friend's house that day with joy in my heart because I wasn't empty on the inside anymore.

My choice to serve God didn't end that day. Every day since then I have had to choose God all over again. I have had to work hard to keep my heart undivided. As you choose to follow God with all of your heart, soul, mind, and strength, you will also have to choose to keep your heart undivided. Staying focused on God and true to Him will help you to pursue the dreams He has for you.

Choice #3: Choose to be totally obedient.

There are two ways to do things: (1) Your Way and (2) God's Way. Which way do you think is the best way? If you said the second way, you are correct.

In reading the entries in this book, you have probably learned by now that God's view of things is very different from ours. He sees the *big picture* while we only see what we've experienced in the past and what we are doing at this very moment.

167

Because He knows and sees everything, He knows how each of our choices will affect the rest of our lives. What seems harmless to us may mess up our opportunity to achieve everything that He has planned for us. Knowing that God's way of doing things is better than ours, we must choose to obey Him in everything we do.

Obedience is the key to achieving all God has for you. If you stay close to Him, keeping an undivided heart, and with His help do everything He asks you to do, you will be amazed as you see His blessing on your life.

Tell about a time when you chose to do things "God's way" and not your own.

....

....

....

As I have already shared with you, I was seventeen when I became a Christian. After choosing to serve God, I discovered that there were many other choices that I had to make. God wanted me to not only give Him my heart for the moment but to give Him my entire future. He asked me in my heart, "Will you follow Me where I'm leading you, (no matter where that is)? Will you prepare for full-time ministry (no matter what you had wanted to do)? Will you let Me use your life now (no matter what people say)?

My friends and family were confused about the changes they saw in me and even discouraged me from pursuing the dreams that God had given me. I felt kind of foolish and disliked the fact that everyone seemed to disapprove. Was I making a huge mistake? Was I "throwing my life away"? As I kept my eyes on God and talked with my youth pastor and his wife, I learned that I could trust God with my present circumstances as well as my future hopes. My youth pastor showed me that I could trust Him with everything.

One passage that really encouraged me then, and still does today, was Proverbs 3:5-6. Look it up and write it down.

God is so trustworthy. He never lies to us, and He always hopes for our best. Because we can trust Him, we should obey Him, believing that He has our best in mind. When God speaks to you about the young man you are dating or the way that you are treating your friends or your parents, He isn't trying to pick on you; He is trying to preserve or keep you so that you will grow to be more like Him. He isn't trying to spoil your fun or mess up your party; He loves you and wants to see all your dreams come true.

When God told me that I was going to be a minister, I was excited. I enrolled in Bethany Bible College and graduated in four years. I was eager to do whatever God had planned for me. It didn't matter to me that I was still single because I was excited about serving God with or without a husband. After almost seven years in full-time ministry (at the time I am writing this), I am still eager to serve Him, but I have often desired to have a husband to serve with.

Several opportunities to date and marry have come my way. At one time I fell in love and even got engaged. Soon I realized that as wonderful as the young man was, he was not the man that God had designed for me. I struggled to end the relationship and tried to bargain with God. *"But God, he loves You. But God, he treats me so well. But God, I love him."*

As God continued to plead with my heart, I realized that if I married the young man, I would be disobeying God and forfeiting the plans He had designed for my life. I would also rob the young man of having God's best for his life. One day I came across a Scripture that pierced my heart. First Samuel 15:22 says, "…To obey is better than sacrifice…." God wanted me to obey His voice.

169

God was merciful and helped us to end the relationship. As painful as it was, God healed our hearts and helped us to remain friends. I am happy to say that later that same year, my friend married God's best choice for his life. What if we hadn't been obedient? Sure, God would have still loved us and may have even blessed our life and ministry together, but it wouldn't have been His *best* plan. Obedience is often difficult, but it yields bountiful rewards.

Reflections

Stop and think. Is there an area of your life that God has asked you to change? Have you been struggling to obey Him? If so, what is it, and why are you having such a hard time being obedient? Write about it. _____

_____

_____

_____

_____

Choices of
the Heart

Part 3

by Jennifer Davis

While attending Bethany Bible College, I heard a story of a young woman who failed to obey God in the choice of her mate. Apparently, God spoke to this woman in her heart when she was just a child and told her that He would one day send her to China to be a missionary. As she grew up, she prayed for the Chinese people and prepared her heart for the day that she would set foot on Chinese soil.

But like most young women, she hoped for a husband, too.

At Bible college she fell in love with a handsome young man. He loved God and treated her well. The only problem was that he didn't want to be a missionary. God spoke to her heart and urged her to obey Him, to choose God's way and not her own. God could see the big picture and knew that this was not His plan. But rather than obey, she chose to marry the young man. She hoped that he would change his mind.

After many years he reluctantly agreed to move to China, but a few short years later he moved his wife and family back to the

United States. The wife was devastated. What about the dreams God had placed in her heart? It was too late to choose obedience. Her window of opportunity had closed. God could still use her life, but it would never be in China.

For many years to come, quiet tears were shed on her pillow each night as she silently wept for China. In her heart the pain was agonizing and overwhelmed her to the point of secretly praying, *God, please remove this burden or remove my husband.* Lack of obedience caused her to miss out on God's best.

In the book of Esther, we read of a beautiful young woman who finds herself wearing a crown. God's hand was on her life, and people favored her greatly because of it. You have probably read the story and know that Esther wasn't born into royalty. In fact, Esther was an orphan who was being raised by her uncle Mordecai. She seemed like a very unlikely candidate for queen. God viewed Esther much differently than maybe you or I would, and allowed the king to favor her.

171

Did He allow Esther to become a queen just so she could wear a crown? No! He had greater purposes in mind. In Esther chapter 2, Mordecai uncovers a great conspiracy. The king's right hand man, Haman, was plotting to destroy the Jewish people. Mordecai and Esther were Jewish. Someone had to stop Haman's evil plan.

Read Esther chapter 4. Mordecai recognized the fact that Esther was the only living person who could influence the king's decision. She had to speak to the king. It was a matter of life and death for all the Jews.

Have you ever found yourself in a situation where you knew that you were the only one who could make things right? What did you do? Explain.

In Esther 4:12-14 Mordecai firmly explained to Esther that if she failed to be obedient to God, He would raise up someone else to deliver the Jews. Wow! Can you imagine the pressure she must have felt? What would *you* have done in her situation? If she went to see the king without his sending for her, she could be killed. If she ignored the information her uncle gave her, an entire race of people would be killed.

Esther 4:14 says: "And who knows but that you have come to royal position for such a time as this?" In other words, the very reason Esther had been made queen was so that she could act in this situation. She had to obey, because God's plan required total obedience.

What feelings and emotions do you think Esther was having as she listened to her uncle's desperate plea? _____

_____

_____

_____

As scared as Esther may have been, she chose to obey. Her heart was undivided, and she desired to serve God no matter where He led her.

God has specific plans for your life, just as He did for Esther.

Write out Ephesians 2:10. _____

_____

_____

If you fail to obey God, He will find someone else to carry out those plans. At times you may feel uncertain as to where He is leading you or why you are in a particular situation. When you feel afraid, quote Proverbs 3:5-6 and choose to trust the Lord. He will help you to obey Him. Would you rather obey and be the one to fulfill His dreams for your life, or would you rather sacrifice those dreams to do things your own way? Choose God's best for your life. Choose to obey.

The Choice Is Yours

God wants the best for your life both now and in the future. No matter what mistakes you have made in the past or the situation you may be entangled in at present, God will help you, lead you, and bless you if you make the right choices:

Choice #1: Choose to serve the Lord.

Choice #2: Choose to have an undivided heart.

Choice #3: Choose to be totally obedient.

Reflections

173

As we saw in the story of Esther, when we choose to obediently serve the Lord with an undivided heart, God beautifully shapes our lives. Do your remember the words that Esther's wise uncle spoke to her? Read Esther 4:14 again and write it down.

_____

_____

_____

God wants your life to become the "greatest story ever told"!

Dare To Dream God's Dream for Your Life

Part 1

by Mark and Suzanne Rentz

Recently, I was asked to speak at a Thanksgiving service. As I looked at my life to find what I was thankful for, something occurred to me. If, as a young girl, I were to have designed my life the way I wanted it to turn out, I could not have planned it as well as God did. I thought I knew what I wanted for my life, but God's plan was above and beyond what I imagined.

I used to dream about being rich and successful. I thought about a dream house and a dream husband along with our dream kids, who never fought, cried, or disobeyed. (Right!) I dreamed we would live happily ever after and ride off into the sunset. Some dream, right? Yet, something was missing. Those dreams were empty, and I knew there was more to my life than success. That's when I stopped living my dream and began living God's.

We talked earlier about a Hebrew woman in the Bible named Esther who, against all odds, became queen and was used by God to save her people. I believe that it is one of the greatest underdog stories in all of Scripture. As a young girl, Esther grew up without her mother and father, raised by her uncle, Mordecai, in a land that was not her own. She understood what it meant to be an outcast and to be discriminated against. But God had a plan for Esther's life that she, even in her wildest imagination, never could have dreamed.

List some of the things that you dream about for your life.

_____

_____

_____

If you could, how would you design your life or your future?

175

_____

_____

_____

As great as those plans may seem, it is vital that you understand that God's dreams for you are far more fulfilling and exciting.

Look up and write Ephesians 3:20.

_____

_____

_____

What are some of the reasons people refuse to dream God's dream for their lives? _____

_____

_____

Look up John 10:10 and describe what kind of life God wants you to lead. What does the word "abundant" mean to you?

God desires you to lead a meaningful and abundant life. Notice I did not say easy, comfortable, or selfish life. He wants you to leave a mark on this planet before you die.

As I look back in my life, I see how God used circumstances and situations to mold and prepare me for His ultimate plan for my life. Friendships, sports, teachers, jobs, school—all were tools in God's hands used to shape me for my future.

We all have dreams. As a little girl, I am sure Esther pretended to be a princess in a palace surrounded by servants. As a teenager I am sure this "princess" dreamed of the prince who would one day whisk her away to safety.

Then one day the impossible became a reality. King Xerxes was searching for a wife. The most beautiful women in the kingdom of Persia were to be presented to the king. Esther was among those chosen. Imagine the excitement and rush of emotions she experienced. Just being chosen as a potential wife was an unbelievable honor. Yet, little did she know that she would be made the king's wife, wear the queen's crown, and save her people from certain destruction.

God had a plan for Esther that was beyond her comprehension. She lived a life that impacted thousands for generations. Why? How? I believe she did all these things because she dared to dream God's dream.

Esther could have allowed fear to keep her from following God's plan. The fear of her past, the fear of failure, or even the fear of death could have prevented her from following God's plan for her life. (See Est. 2:5-7; 4:9-11.)

Throughout our lives, God is continually preparing us for our future. Sometimes these preparations are painful and hard to understand. During these low points, we are tempted to doubt God and His ability to see us through. We may even think He has given up on us. No! Nothing is further from the truth.

Reflections

Write out Romans 8:28. _____

_____

_____

God has not forsaken us; Romans 8:28 tells us that He works out everything for good to those who love Him and are called according to His purpose.

177

Read and write out Proverbs 3:5-6. _____

_____

_____

What does it mean to trust someone? _____

_____

_____

Read James 1:2-4. What does James say trials will produce in your life? _____

_____

_____

Dare To Dream God's Dream for Your Life

Part 2

by Mark and Suzanne Rentz

I want to encourage you to set aside some time and read the story of Joseph's life in Genesis chapters 36-50. This is an incredible story of how God used horrible and unfair circumstances to shape a young man with dreams and to save a nation.

Sometimes it is hard to trust God with our dreams when things are tough, but He sees things from an eternal perspective. Throughout our lives God shapes and molds us in preparation for our future. It is as if we are driving a car. We can look out of the windows and see the road in front of us, but our view is limited. We don't know what is a mile ahead, but God's view is not limited. He sees the road we are on and the freeway we are approaching.

Because of our limited view, we often see only our circumstances and don't always understand where we are headed. Unlike us, God sees the whole picture and wants us to face life trusting Him. With this in mind, do you think we should trust ourselves on the road, or should we trust the One who knows our final destination?

God is faithful to do what He said He will in His Word. All of life's problems and difficulties will produce a life that has proved the faithfulness of God.

What negative circumstances or events have you experienced that God has used to prepare you for your future?

_____

_____

_____

What good did He bring out of a negative experience?

_____

_____

I recently came across a short story that illustrates how much we can trust our heavenly Father with every part of our lives.

"As the little girl curled up on her bed, she clutched her porcelain doll close to her heart. She treasured her doll more than anything else. Lying on her bed, she gently stroked the doll's cheek, embracing it with love.

"A deep but gentle voice echoed in the girl's ear. She recognized it as being the voice of her father, calling her to come to him. Eager to respond, she jumped off her bed. As she slid to the floor, her most precious treasure slipped out of her grasp, crashing against the hardwood floor.

"The little girl looked on in horror as her doll's face shattered to pieces. Collapsing beside her broken treasure, she tried desperately to collect the shattered remains lying before her. The father came to his child's bedside and knelt down beside her. Wrapping his arm around her shoulders to draw her close to him, he gently consoled her. With his other arm he carefully placed a new porcelain doll in his daughter's tender grasp. As she gazed up at her father, beams of joy shone through her downcast eyes.

"Watching his child lovingly cradle her new treasure, the father's heart overflowed with contentment. He had always known his daughter would love the doll he had chosen for her, yet time and time again she had refused to accept it, holding on to her treasure, not realizing that his was better. Now, as her treasure lay shattered before her, she was in a position to accept his precious gift."[1]

Finally, how do we discover God's dream for our lives? First of all, I want to encourage you that God wants you to know His dream for your life more than you do. He is more committed to seeing you succeed and fulfill all that He has for you than you are.

What does each Scripture below have to say?

Philippians 1:6

Ephesians 2:10

Jeremiah 29:11

He *will* complete what He has begun in you. So, relax and trust that God has a plan, a future, and a dream for your life. Know that He is preparing and processing you right now so that you will faithfully accomplish His dreams. Ask Him; God will reveal to you all you need to know in His timing.

Reflections

In your own words, how do these Scriptures apply to you?

Matthew 6:33 _____

_____

_____

Jeremiah 33:3 _____

_____

_____

Romans 12:1,2 _____

_____

_____

How do these Scriptures tell us we learn the will of God?

181

_____

_____

So often we hold on to our own dreams and desires, treasuring them more than anything else, when God wants to give us His dreams and desires. If our dreams don't line up with God's dreams, we will never be fulfilled, and we will be left unsatisfied. But when our dreams do line up with God's, we will experience true fulfillment. Take God's hand, and He will lead you; your life will never be more exciting.

Esther's Secret

by Erin E. Zonio

In January 1992, the doctor's diagnosis came back that I had a rare, genetic, degenerative disease called *Pseudoxanthoma Elasticum,* or more easily referred to as P.X.E. Not knowing the severity of the condition, my mind began to race: *But I want to be a missionary! What about my dream of working in ministry? I want to have a family! I'm so young! What's going to happen? How much longer am I going to live?* I visited another doctor to find out more about P.X.E. and was told it could cause blindness or one of my main arteries could break open. There are no cures; my health problems could only be corrected as they occurred.

My future seemed bleak. I felt I could not make any plans, and I could not hope. Should I even think about getting married or having children, or would I end up dying and leaving my husband to raise our child alone? Who knew if I would still be alive at the age of thirty? How would God complete His plan through me?

It's been several years since that diagnosis, and occasionally I do lapse into anxiety and worry. However, I know that everyone has uncertainties in their life; everyone has insecurities that cause them to question their capability to fulfill God's plan for them. But that doesn't mean that we shrink away from following Him and do not walk in His plan for us.

We have been looking at the book of Esther in the Bible that tells the story of Queen Esther. She was a woman God had called, yet she had every reason to back down from God's call. She had every reason to fear the future, but she did not allow fear, anxiety, or uncertainty to paralyze her. What was the secret she was hiding? She was a Jew.

While the Jews were in captivity, King Xerxes wanted a new wife, a new queen, so he called together many beautiful women; from them he would make his choice.

At her uncle Mordecai's urging, Esther disguised her identity and went to the king's palace to begin beauty treatments. From the beginning, she stood out from among the others. When the king saw her, he immediately took an interest in her, and after a series of events, King Xerxes chose Esther to be his queen. However, no one knew that Esther was Jewish.

Jews were despised by the people of this culture. When Esther's uncle refused to bow to one of the king's top men, it was not difficult for the king to agree to their destruction. I believe that if King Xerxes had known Esther's secret, he surely would not have chosen her.

But did Esther back down from the call for a queen? No, she confidently responded—and was chosen.

God Has a Plan for Your Life...

What are some dreams you wish to accomplish?

Jeremiah 29:11 says, "'For I know the plans I have for you,' declares the Lord, 'plans to prosper you and not to harm you, plans to give you hope and a future.'"

Have you begun to see God's plan for your life yet? If so, what is it? _____

_____

_____

_____

Mordecai pointed out to Esther that God had a plan for her when he said, "And who knows but that you have come to royal position for such a time as this?" (Est. 4:14). God had been guiding her and leading her up to that point, and He would continue to do so.

...Even If It Seems Impossible.

Whenever we are striving to fulfill God's purpose for us, we will be confronted with the realization that we are not qualified. There will always be something in our lives that causes us to doubt that God really can use us. We are weak and inadequate. Esther was a Jew; how could she be a queen?

Below are some Scriptures describing people whom God used; each one had an area of insecurity in their life. Complete the following chart:

184

Scripture	Name	Insecurity	How God Used Them
Exodus 3:7-10; 4:10-12			
Genesis 15:5; Romans 4:18,19			
Judges 6:11-15			

What are some things about you and your life that make you believe God can't *possibly* use you?

God knows who you are, and He has not given you dreams only to disappoint you. God has not called you just to leave you feeling discouraged. He knew all the facts when He called you, when He made a promise to you. He knows your history, your heritage, and where you are now, and you are the one He's called—even with all your shortcomings.

Reflections

Read Romans 4:18-21. What did Abraham do when he realized how "silly" God's promise seemed to be? _____

_____

185

_____

What happened as a result? _____

_____

_____

Read and write out Ephesians 2:10. _____

_____

_____

If Esther had not been a Jew, the Jewish nation would not have had a friend in the palace. They would have been annihilated. Esther's Jewish heritage could have been a source of shame and insecurity, but because she did not back away from God's plan, she became an instrument of God's salvation and deliverance for the Jewish people.

Write down any words of encouragement that God has spoken to you through this chapter. _____

_____

Excellence—

God's Standard

by Erin E. Zonio

About ten years ago, the movie *Bill and Ted's Excellent Adventure* was released. These two teenage, time-traveling dudes had a favorite word that they used as an adjective, an adverb, and for any other purpose they could find. Maybe it was just my friend Roy, but it seemed everybody was using Bill and Ted's word for a while, and I can still hear the way they said it: *Excellent!* Bill and Ted and all their fans used the word in the same way they also said *cool* and *awesome,* and the way we might say *tight, phat,* or *sweet.*

Sadly, excellence is not a quality that marks our society today. Because of past situations, many people feel that some areas of our national government cannot be trusted. In our own communities, there are a suprising number of people who don't put forth very much effort at work or at school. Morally, many people have decided, "What's best for you may not be best for me." We are seen as intolerant or judgmental if we suggest that others are going against God's law or if we claim that there is only one God.

While some of the neighbors, friends, and authority figures in our lives have chosen not to establish a standard, it is very important that we, as Christians, determine to establish a right and a wrong. It is imperative that we draw a line between what is approved of and disapproved of by God. Sin is not relative, as our society claims.

Philippians 2:9-10 says, "And this I pray, that your love may abound still more and more in knowledge and all discernment *that you may approve the things that are excellent,* that you may be sincere and without offense till the day of Christ." God commands us to set a standard of excellence in our lives.

What is it?

Excellence could be defined as superiority; exalted merit; virtue.

How does our society define excellence? _____

_____

_____

How do your friends define excellence? _____

187

_____

_____

The word *excellent* is also used in the Bible to describe God and everything He did; it's used to describe His power and love. However, *excellent* does not only describe God; it also describes how our behavior and things in our lives should be. The New Testament was originally written in Greek, and the Greek word for *excellent* is *diaphero,* which means to surpass, to be better, to differ from, to be of more value.[1]

In light of this, how do you think God defines excellence?

_____

_____

Name someone you think lives a life of excellence and describe why. _____

_____

_____

Jesus was the most excellent person to ever live on earth. While many of the leaders of His day were accused of being hypocrites (teaching one thing and doing another), no one could ever accuse Christ of that, no matter how many times they tried. He was humble, He was honest, and He could be trusted. He never hurt anyone, even unintentionally, but was always looking out for the good of others. He completed everything God asked Him to do, even when it was as difficult as dying on the cross. He loved everyone sincerely. Anyone who got to know Jesus knew He was different.

The ultimate example of excellence is Jesus, so our standard of excellence means that we do our absolute best to be like Jesus in everything we do, say, or think. How can you accomplish that?

1. Renew your mind.

Romans 12:2 says, "Do not conform any longer to the pattern of this world, but be transformed by the renewing of your mind...." To change our behavior, we need to start by changing the way we think. It's our minds that tell us what to say and how to behave. There is a saying: *Garbage in, garbage out.* If our minds are full of things that are ungodly, not Christlike, and less than excellent, that is how we are going to behave.

*Read Philippians 4:8. What are the attributes of things we should be putting into our minds?*_____

_____

_____

What are some sources of things that are not excellent?

_____

_____

2. Recognize who you are and who you aren't.

There are many places in the Bible that list the behavior of both Christians and non-Christians. If you are a Christian, you have been set free from living the way the rest of the world lives. You do not *have* to sin anymore; you have a choice now.

Read Colossians 3:5-17. Based upon this passage, list below the characteristics of "who you are" and "who you aren't" in the appropriate columns.

Who You Are   Who You Aren't

_____

189

_____

_____

_____

_____

3. Look to Jesus for strength.

We cannot be perfect on our own. In fact, the Bible tells us that our attempts at being perfect are just as unclean as filthy rags. (See Isa. 64:6.) The apostle Paul dealt with this. Read 2 Corinthians 12:7-10 to see what Paul learned.

Read John 15:4-8. How can you "abide" in Jesus? _____

_____

_____

_____

4. Remember that excellence is a process.

Excellence is not synonymous with perfection. While God commands us to be holy, He knows we will fall short many times. However, He also expects us to do things to the best of our ability and to continue to try.

Paul was a great man of God, but even he failed sometimes. In Philippians 3:12-14 he writes, "Not that I have already obtained all this, or have already been made perfect, but I press on to take hold of that for which Christ Jesus took hold of me. Brothers [and sisters], I do not consider myself yet to have taken hold of it. But one thing I do: Forgetting what is behind and straining toward what is ahead, I press on toward the goal to win the prize for which God has called me heavenward in Christ Jesus."

Remember that God knows exactly where you are in this process of becoming like Jesus. He is merciful, and He wants to help you accomplish it.

Reflections

Take some time to evaluate the standards you have set in your life and to evaluate if you are holding to those standards.

What attributes of Christ do you see in your life? _____

_____

_____

_____

What characteristics of Jesus do others see? _____

_____

_____

_____

Do you feel that you are really "rising above" the standards of your peers, or are you compromising? _____

_____

_____

_____

What are some areas in which you need to start applying excellence? _____

_____

_____

_____

What can you do (practically speaking) to apply excellence to those areas? _____

191

_____

_____

_____

Worth the Wait

Part 1

by Rebecca Simmons

In junior high school, my greatest desire was for a boyfriend. All my friends were in and out of relationships, and that was all I thought of. I was really looking forward to the day I would be allowed to date. At the time I am writing this, I'm 17 and I have never been kissed. In fact, I have not dated or had a boyfriend either. I have chosen a different route than the one that at one time seemed so appealing.

Now, how did this change come about when boys were always on my mind? At a youth conference, the speaker challenged us to commit one year to God. This meant that through the next year, we would not date or get involved in a relationship, but would focus on God. *A year?* I thought, *No way, that's too long!* So I crossed out the part of the commitment form that said "one year" and wrote in "six months." That marked the beginning of a commitment that has now lasted five years.

What Do You Desire?

As a young woman like you, I know, understand, and feel much of what you may be experiencing. I am not exempt from the same desires for intimacy and security just because I have chosen not to date at this point in my life. You're probably wondering why I would make such an extreme choice.

It is because I have found another option. As I watched many of my friends get hurt as they jumped from relationship to relationship, I sensed that there must be an alternative to this cycle of bliss and pain they kept experiencing. There is an alternative, and it is found in Isaiah 58:11.

Read the verse and write what it means to you.

_____

_____

_____

Before I could be content in what God had for me, I had to first learn to be satisfied in Him alone. I could not possibly be satisfied in God if I were seeking out ways to fulfill my own desires. When I laid those desires for intimacy, security, and understanding before the Lord, I was more than satisfied. I found God to be not only the most fulfilling, but also the most romantic part of my life.

It is natural for us, as young women, to desire intimacy, understanding, and unconditional love. God placed these desires in our hearts when He created us, and everything God creates is good. However, these good desires can actually cause grief if they are not cared for properly. This is where many young women stumble and get hurt: They look to a man to satisfy their desires for intimacy, understanding, and unconditional love, and they are disappointed.

Where, or in whom, have you searched for intimacy, under-standing, and unconditional love? What was the result?

_____

_____

_____

Flowers for My Love

Until we first learn to be satisfied in God, we will never be satisfied in a relationship, not even marriage. God alone can satisfy us completely. I made a statement earlier that God is romantic. I know we do not often think of Him as such, but He truly is. Only He can completely fulfill all our desires. No man is capable of such a feat.

When I stopped looking for a relationship to fulfill my desire and I allowed God to satisfy me, I was content. However, my being content in God did not mean that my desires for a relationship disappeared. In fact, it was quite the contrary. Not only has God satisfied me, but He has given me hope, expectancy, and dreams for the future.

Being satisfied in God is a choice we have to make daily. It is easy for us to get distracted with a situation or circumstance and take our focus off of Him and place it on ourselves. It is in these times that we become vulnerable to feelings of self-pity and loneliness.

194

I experienced this one day as I was driving home; my body began to shake with sobs, and my eyes blurred with tears. I felt hurt because no one seemed to understand what I was feeling. Upon returning from my visit to North Central Bible College, I was bursting with excitement. My whole future seemed to be somehow wrapped up in that school, but no one seemed to care. I was dying for someone to understand or even just listen to my excitement, but no one did.

Driving home, feeling hurt and lonely, I began to notice some flowers growing in the field alongside the road. As I gazed at them, my heart was filled with peace and contentment. Though I felt lonely, I was not alone. I had just been so wrapped up in my own pain that I could not hear God calling my name. It took a field of flowers to catch my attention. When I turned my focus to God, He told me (in my heart), "Just as a man would bring flowers to the woman he loves, so have I created these flowers for you. They are a symbol of My love."

God knows our hearts. He is able to give us all we need to be content. The author of the book of Lamentations in the Bible expressed this beautifully when he wrote, "…The Lord is my portion; therefore I will wait for Him" (Lam. 3:24). When we learn to first be satisfied in God alone, then we will experience the greatest amounts of joy and fulfillment in the life He has for us.

An Equation You Won't Find in Algebra

Untarnished, untainted, immaculate, spotless, chaste, virtuous, clean, unblemished, absolute, innocent—*What in the world is she talking about?* you may be thinking. Well, I'm describing something or someone that is pure. Purity is something that must be fought for. It will not be won easily. But how do we fight for purity? Does it mean we can't date or hang out with guys? No, not necessarily. Whether we choose to date or not to date, we are all called to the same standard of purity in relationships. What is that standard? Let's see.

195

God never said, "Thou shalt not date," but He did say, "Delight yourself in the Lord and He will give you the desires of your heart." This verse is found in Psalm 37:4. Look it up and read through verse 7. While you're reading, see if you can find the conditions (in other words, God will do what, if we will do what).

Did you find the conditions? God said that He would give us the desires of our hearts and make our righteousness shine like the dawn *if* we delight in Him, commit our ways to Him, and trust in Him. Then, in verse 7, we are told to "Be still before the Lord and wait patiently for Him…."

Reflections

Take a few minutes and write out what it means to you in the area of guy/girl relationships, to…

1. Delight ourselves in the Lord. _____

_____

_____

_____

2. Commit our ways to Him. _____

_____

_____

3. Trust in Him. _____

_____

4. Wait patiently for Him. _____

_____

_____

Here is an equation I have found helpful to me in pursuing God's will for my life: delight + commit + trust + wait = man of your dreams.

By delighting in the Lord, committing our ways to Him, trusting in Him, and waiting patiently for Him, we choose to joyfully accept and follow the plans He has for us. It means that we make Him our first priority; we place His will above our desires. The more I learn to do this, the more I am finding out how incredibly awesome God's plan is. His plans for me are exceeding my own. As you embark on the second part of this devotion, I'd like to challenge you to apply this equation to your life, too.

Worth the Wait

Part 2

by Rebecca Simmons

"My Knight in Shining Armor"

"Delight yourself in the Lord...."

Is this a familiar scenario to you?

"Oh Jen, you'll never believe the guy I just met! He's so sweet, and he totally goes out of his way to take care of me. I have never felt so special in my entire life! Oh, and get this—today, while I was in history class, he stood outside waiting for me, and every time I glanced at him, I found him gazing back at me. I could hardly wait for the class to end so I could see him again!"

Maybe you've experienced this same excitement of having a crush on someone or of someone's having a crush on you. What's it like? Exhilarating? Blissful? Breathtaking? Now, what would you say if I told you that this is how God feels about you?

My last statement may have caught you off guard, but it's true. God delights in you. What does it mean to "delight" in something or someone?

Write out your definition of "delight." _____

_____

_____

To delight in someone or something is to find great joy or pleasure in that person or thing. So, if God delights in you, then He finds great pleasure and joy in you. Like the man in the scenario, God finds pleasure in just being near you and spending time with you.

Read and write out Zephaniah 3:17. _____

_____

_____

Isn't it exciting when someone likes you, and he goes out of his way to please you? Of course it is, but place yourself in that person's shoes for a moment. Let's say you had a crush on this guy; we'll call him Matt. Every time you see Matt your heart beats a little faster, and your palms begin to sweat. He's everything you ever wanted in a guy. Now, what would make this relationship more exciting and meaningful? If he liked you back, right?

Let me ask you another question: Do you delight in God as much as He delights in you? Are your thoughts constantly on Him? Is He all you talk about? Do you look forward to getting away and spending time with Him alone?

Let's make it our prayer and our desire to learn to delight in God as much as He delights in us. I believe that as we seek to delight in Him, we will see our relationship with Him begin to blossom. This happens when we spend time in His Presence, getting to know who He is. The more we get to know who He is, the more we'll become like Him. We will learn to delight in Him as He delights in us, and His desires will become our desires.

I'm With You All the Way

"…commit your ways to the Lord…."

"Get on the line!" my coach barked. Grudgingly, I jogged toward the baseline with the rest of my basketball team. We had messed up the drill once again, and our punishment was to run another "suicide" run. "Okay, you have twenty-seven seconds. Go!" We took off sprinting as fast as we could—to the free-throw line and back, half court and back, opposite free-throw line and back, opposite baseline and "5…4…." We struggled to keep our legs going faster, faster. "…3…2…." Almost there. Hurry! "1!" Panting for breath, we collided with the wall—an abrupt but welcome halt. We had made it.

Then came the lecture from coach. "We have a big game tomorrow. In order to get to the play-offs, we must beat Castilleja! I don't want to see any more messing around out there. Pay attention…work hard!"

I heard this speech often during my sophomore year of high school. A high standard had been set for the girls' varsity basketball team at Fremont Christian. We were expected to be good, disciplined players. Though none of us were truly great players, we were an incredible team; we were committed to our coach and to each other; we played hard because we practiced hard.

What makes a great team, a great athlete? Commitment. There is a quote written on the wall of our school gym that says, "The will to succeed is important, but the will to prepare is vital." How can we expect to succeed if we are not willing to prepare? We must be committed in the time of preparation if we want to succeed in the game. This is true in relationships as well as in sports.

Who do you believe our "coach" is as Christians? How does He coach us in the area of relationships? _____

_____

_____

God wants to see us experience the greatest amount of fulfillment in the perfect relationship He has for us. In order for this to happen, He will coach us until we are ready for "the big game." Like every good coach, God has a playbook—the Bible. In this book, He gives us the instructions we need in order to be victorious in the area of relationships. Let's take a look at some of His instructions.

Read each passage, and then write the main point on the line below the reference.

1 Thessalonians 4:3-8 _____

_____

Titus 2:12 _____

_____

Psalm 119:9-11 _____

_____

Isaiah 52:9-12 _____

_____

Matthew 5:8 _____

_____

1 Timothy 5:22 _____

_____

Hebrews 13:4,5 _____

_____

In essence, we are called to live a pure life. How do we do this?

It all comes down to choices—God's will or ours. This is where we must choose to commit our ways to God. When we commit our ways to Him, we take on His will and His desires. It is *simple*, in that all we must do is choose to obey Him, but it is not always *easy*.

God's will for me was not to date during this period of my life, but to focus wholly on Him. In doing this, I have experienced a wonderful, intimate relationship with God, and He has enabled me to minister in ways I never thought possible. But that is just me. God has not called everyone not to date. But whether we choose to date or we choose to wait, we are called to the same standard of purity. God, our coach, wants to see us succeed; but in order for that to happen, we must stay in the safe pasture.

Reflections

Read Psalm 37:3. Where is the "safe pasture"? _____

_____

_____

When we are in obedience to God, we are under His protection. It is when we step out of His will that we are subject to the consequences of sin. We often hear of sexually-transmitted diseases and pregnancy—the major consequences of impurity. But what about the consequences of emotional intimacy outside of God's plans?

Many young women experience heartache and depression as a result of broken relationships. God never intended for His daughters to experience this pain, but it is a consequence of choosing their will over His. Before we take another step, let's commit our ways to the Lord and choose to obey. He knows which plays to call.

201

Worth the Wait

Part 3

by Rebecca Simmons

Are You Serious?

"...trust in Him...."

Let me tell you about a young woman in Genesis 24 in the Bible who trusted God so much that she was willing to do whatever He asked. Her name was Rebekah, and she probably was not much older than many of us. Try to put yourself in her shoes as I tell you her story.

It was a day like every other in Rebekah's hometown as she hurriedly prepared for her daily trip to the spring. Dusk was drawing near, and she had to get back before dark. Besides, she had spent all day in the house, cooking and sewing with her mother, and she was ready to get out for a bit. As she drew near the spring, she noticed a man standing with a group of camels. *No bother,* she thought, *Travelers often pass through here.* So, she went down and filled her jar, but as she came back up, she noticed the traveler approaching her.

"Miss," he called, "may I please have some water from your jar?"

"Yes," she replied to this weary traveler. Then she noticed that his camels also appeared to be thirsty, so she added, "I'll draw water for your camels, also." At this, the man began to take out expensive jewelry and give it to her. What a shock that must have been for Rebekah! This man she did not know was giving her jewelry and acting as though he knew her. He even asked if her parents could put him up for the night. In her surprise, she ran home to tell her family. Once they heard her story, they invited the man home for dinner. It was then that God's plan for Rebekah began to unfold.

It turned out that this man was a servant of Abraham, Rebekah's great uncle, and he wanted her to go back to Canaan with him to marry Abraham's son, Isaac. What must have been going through Rebekah's head at that moment? *What's that, God? You want me to leave my home and my country to marry a man I have never met? But…okay.* She trusted.

Rebekah trusted God in two incredible ways. The first was her trust in God to fulfill her desires. Rebekah was going about her daily routine the day God's plan unfolded before her. She was not looking for a relationship or for marriage, though I'm certain she must have desired it. In fact, she probably heard all the latest news of who was betrothed to whom and wondered when her day would come, but still, she trusted.

Then, without warning, her day arrived. A man came who wanted to take her to a faraway land she had never heard of to marry a man she had never met. And what was her reply? "I will go." Again, she trusted.

Are we willing to trust God to the same extent Rebekah did? Are we trusting God to one day unite us with the man He has for us, or are we impatiently seeking out something to satisfy us at present?

One night as I was praying, I began to pour all my desires out before the Lord. As I did this, He spoke these words to my heart: "I know your desires, and I want to fulfill them, but take what I have for you now." Just because God doesn't always give us what we want when we want it, doesn't mean He's forgotten our desires. It just means He has something different for us at present.

God knew Rebekah's desires, and His plan for her life was in action far before she knew what was happening. What do you think would have happened if Rebekah had decided to go to town to see the tentmaker's son instead of taking care of her task of drawing water from the well? She might have missed out on God's plan for her life, but she didn't. She did what God had for her, and He fulfilled her desires.

Reflections

Hang on a Minute

"…wait patiently for Him…."

Let's look back at what we have learned so far. We learned that before we could be in any relationship, we must first be satisfied in God. We are satisfied in Him when we learn to delight in Him. Then we discovered the secret to living a life of purity: committing our ways to the Lord and choosing to obey. And finally, we determined how we could trust God in the area of relationships. Now, it's time to wait.

"What? Wait?" you may ask. Yes, "Be still before the Lord and wait patiently for him…." That's what Psalm 37:7 says. This is probably the most difficult step of all. You may be wondering if all of this is worth it. The sacrifices are big; is the blessing worth it? I don't know. Let's ask the bride.

The large, ornate doors swing open; music drifts into the hall where she stands. She glances toward the altar and there he waits, the man she has dreamed of her entire life. Full of anticipation, she glides down the aisle, all the while gazing into his loving eyes. Silently, he waits. Their gaze, so tender, embarrasses even the most inquisitive of onlookers.

Each step carries her closer to the fulfillment of this seemingly endless dream. It has been a long while. But today, her wait would come to an end, and she would belong to him. She would give him everything: her heart, her life, her undying devotion. She has saved it all for him.

A few steps more and she would be at his side. Now, one step. She stands beside him. He takes her arm; their fingers entwine, and their eyes lock upon each other's. Time seems to freeze as their eyes speak words that could be heard by no other: "I loved you before I knew you; I waited; I trusted. Now I am yours forever."

Is it worth it?

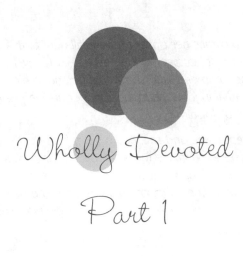

Wholly Devoted

Part 1

Staying Pure

I love rainy days. While dark skies, wet weather, and icy winds aren't fun to walk to school in, they have always helped me to slow down and relax a little.

When I was in college, rainy days were the best days. After morning chapel the students and faculty would hang out in the "D.C." (Dining Commons) and laugh with friends as we sipped hot cocoa or coffee. I remember how all of the windows would fog up because the temperature inside was so much warmer than the temperature outside. Rainy days remind me of hot soup, warm drinks, cozy fires, and bad hair. (There's a down side to everything.)

As I am writing this, it is a rainy day. Outside, El Nino is raging. Inside, I am safe, warm, dry, and reflective. There's something about a rainy day that makes people stop and think, dream, reflect. On days like that, I often think about what God has done in my life, from where He has brought me, and to where He is leading me.

Stop and reflect a little:

From where has God brought you? (What is your testimony? How did you become a Christian? How have you changed? Grown?)

_____

_____

_____

_____

Where is He leading you? (Has God shared with you the plans He has for you? Have you sensed His direction for your life? Who do you hope to be? What do you hope to be doing?)

_____

_____

_____

207

As you will discover (if you haven't already), all of the entries in this devotional are designed to convince you that you are unique and special. Our heavenly Father has created you in His image for a very special reason and purpose. You have been designed *For Such a Time as This.*

Knowing and understanding this truth is so important. So many people spend their lives searching for meaning and purpose. In an attempt to "find themselves" they often lose sight of who they really are.

God views you as a precious treasure. You are a daughter whose worth is priceless. His desire is to help you discover who you really are in His eyes and then teach you to live your life in a manner that reflects that truth.

Several years ago a movie entitled "Anastasia" was released that illustrated how someone's life is transformed when she discovers her true identity.

Anastasia was a Russian princess whose royal family was assassinated when she was just a young girl. Because of their deaths, Anastasia was forced to flee for her life. Raised by a peasant woman, Anastasia grew up totally unaware of who she really was, of her royal lineage.

As a young adult, she struggled to find her true identity. It wasn't until she was reunited with her wealthy grandmother in Paris that she realized the life she had was worthy of living. She was a princess, not a peasant. While Anastasia chose to walk away from her new life and social standing, she would always carry with her the knowledge of her true identity.

We too are princesses, not peasants. The King (Father God) loves us desperately and wants us to love Him in return. He desires for us to be wholly devoted to Him and to live our lives in a manner that pleases Him. This devotional was designed to help you commit to live your life in that manner, not serving God with part of your heart or effort, but to truly be *Wholly Devoted.*

Every movie has a villain of some kind. Anastasia's villain, Rasputin, an evil, demon-possessed sorcerer, tried at every turn to destroy Anastasia and prevent her from discovering her true identity. You and I have a very real enemy who, like Rasputin, wants to destroy us. Satan, the devil, is committed to destroying your life while preventing you from discovering your true identity in Christ.

Write out John 10:10. _____

_____

Satan will stop at nothing to distract you from fulfilling God's plans for your life. He will tempt you, discourage you, depress you, and eventually destroy you if you don't keep your focus on God. By making a commitment to remain wholly devoted to God, you must do your best to (1) stay pure and (2) guard your heart. When you choose to be wholly devoted, you choose to preserve God's best plan for your life. If you choose not to be wholly devoted, you choose to become an easy target for the enemy of your soul.

Wholly Devoted To Staying Pure

The word *pure* is used to describe many things: *pure* silk, *pure* gold, *pure* milk chocolate, to name a few.

When you hear people say to "stay pure," what do you think they are talking about? _____

_____

_____

To be pure is to be spotless, stainless, free from harshness or roughness.[1] Often when we are in church and we hear people use the word *pure,* we immediately think they are referring to sexual purity. While it is definitely true that we must commit to remaining sexually pure, I have learned that staying pure involves much more than that.

Staying pure is more than just making a commitment to say and do all the right things. It is a commitment to show God, through your thoughts and actions, that He is the most important part of your life. It is to be wholly devoted to Him in everything you do.

In the Sermon on the Mount, Jesus taught that the pure in heart will see God. (See Matt. 5:8.) He was referring to those whose attitudes and motives of the heart (along with actions) were totally spotless and stainless before God.

How would you define "heart"? _____

_____

_____

_____

_____

How would you define motives and attitudes? _____

_____

_____

_____

They say that your heart is the real you—the core of who you are. Because there is so much pressure on young women to look and act a certain way, many girls learn at an early age to hide their real hearts behind masks. Their masks are designed to protect them from feeling the pain of rejection.

How do you feel about yourself? Have you ever felt like you were hiding behind a mask? Why do you think you have to wear a mask? Write your responses down. _____

_____

_____

_____

_____

Young woman, God sees and knows the real you. He knows your thoughts and feelings. He knows the condition of your heart. He sees behind your mask.

Read Proverbs 5:21-23. The Bible tells us that our "ways are in full view of the Lord…." God knows all and sees all, including the acts done in the strictest secrecy. Let's put it this way: He's even read your diary. As a matter of fact, He even knows the things you haven't written down for fear that someone might read them. He has read the diary of your heart.

As God views your heart today, at this moment, do you feel He has found a heart that is wholly devoted to Him? Have you made a wholehearted attempt to "stay pure"? Explain. _____

_____

_____

As God reads our hearts, He sees not only our actions but He views the *motives* of our hearts. Motives are the driving force behind all of our actions. You see, a motive is a need or desire in your life that causes you to act and respond as you do. In every situation we can be motivated by our desire to please God or motivated to please others or motivated to please ourselves. Whenever we choose to simply please ourselves or others, Satan is pleased, too. Whenever we allow God's Holy Spirit to motivate us, God is pleased, and our enemy is defeated!

To remain pure we must allow our love for God to determine how we act. Our love for God and our desire to please Him should motivate us to "stay pure," making choices that will reflect who God is.

211

Reflections

Describe a time when you made a choice or responded to someone in a way that didn't please God.

Think about your motives in that situation. What was the "driving force" behind your action?

Psychology teaches that all behavior is the result of hidden foundations, and that all of our words are the expressions of thoughts. That sounds similar to Matthew 12:34, "From out of the overflow of the heart the mouth speaks." This is how it works:

Your thoughts—lead to your actions—lead to your feelings.

One step leads to the other. If you commit to "stay pure" in your thoughts and motives, your feelings and actions will be pure. Choose to be wholly devoted to staying pure.

Wholly Devoted

Part 2

Guarding Your Heart

by Jennifer Davis

In order to be wholly devoted to God, you must make a commitment to stay pure. Staying pure requires you to be wholly devoted to guarding your heart.

Read Proverbs 4:20-27 out loud. Write out Proverbs 4:23:

_____

_____

*What do you think this verse means?*_____

_____

_____

When I first read Proverbs 4:23, I immediately thought it meant that I needed to harden my heart in order to protect myself from getting hurt. Many people believe that by hardening or desensitizing their hearts, they are guarding themselves from unwanted or undeserved pain. They do this by putting protective shells around their hearts and pushing everyone away. What they wind up doing is preventing themselves from receiving or giving love. This is not what the author of Proverbs intended for us to do.

The word "heart" in this verse is used to describe a person's feelings, will, and intellect. Remember, your heart is the real you. Proverbs 4:23 instructs us to actively monitor what we allow into our hearts because it will affect who we are.

The expression "garbage in—garbage out" has already been mentioned, but because we want our lives to reflect a heart wholly devoted to God, we must carefully guard what influences us. The friends we have, the books and magazines we read, the movies and TV shows we watch, the music we listen to, the Web sites and chat rooms we go into all affect who we are. We really need to take this verse to heart and remember that "we are what we read, watch, listen to, and hang around." The bottom line is, be careful.

Jesus spoke of the necessity of guarding your heart when He showed that the heart of a person was the source of their thoughts and actions.

Read Matthew 15:18-19. The source of trouble or blessing is found in the contents of your heart. I learned this the hard way when I was in college.

During my junior year at Bethany Bible College, I failed to guard my heart and allowed jealousy to take root. There was a really great new student who seemed to be perfect in every way. Instead of reaching out to her and making a new friend, I opted to feel insecure about myself and to become jealous of her. I listened to the enemy who told me that I wasn't as valuable as she was (when we listen to Satan's lies, we set ourselves up to become insecure). Because I allowed jealousy to become a part of the foundation of my heart, my behavior and words were affected.

Suddenly, I struggled to even talk to or look at the new girl. I constantly compared myself to her, and in my eyes, I never measured up. I felt like a total loser. I went out of my way to avoid her and even allowed other friendships to suffer in order to keep my distance from her. The jealousy ruled my heart. I was miserable. If I had guarded my heart and talked to God about my feelings, things could have been much different.

It wasn't until I finally gave in and asked God to help me and forgive me that my sin of jealousy was uprooted, and I was free to be her friend.

Describe a time when you failed to "guard your heart." _____

_____

_____

I allowed jealousy to "take root" in my heart. Examine your heart. What sins, if any, do you see rooted in your heart?

_____

_____

*How have these secret sins affected your behavior?*_____

_____

_____

Stop now and ask God to forgive you and to uproot these sins from your heart.

We can't expect to do or watch anything and to go anywhere we feel like and still have a "pure heart." We must actively take steps each day to guard our hearts and remain wholly devoted to God.

Here is a quick list of steps to take that I hope will help you to guard your heart.

1. Flee from youthful desires.

Write out 2 Timothy 2:22. _____

_____

_____

This verse instructs us to free ourselves from situations that promote compromise. For example, if you are trying to stay pure in your relationship with your boyfriend, don't sit on the couch together in the dark—unless your parents are sitting between you. Use wisdom and guard your heart.

Write out James 4:7. _____

_____

_____

If you read Genesis 39, you will find the story of Joseph and Potiphar's wife. Joseph knew how to resist the devil. Joseph fled when he was confronted with sin because he desired a pure heart. Learn to do the same. Joseph was fleeing to avoid having premarital sexual relations. If your boyfriend doesn't share your standard of purity and you want to "flee youthful desires," then you may need to break off your relationship with him. He'll only take you where you don't want to go and do things you don't want to do.

Remember the old saying, "If you play with matches, you'll get burned."

2. Be accountable to someone.

To be accountable is to be responsible or be answerable to someone. When you are accountable to someone, you choose to explain willingly your motives and actions to that person, to answer to that person.

Find a friend with whom you can grow spiritually. Make a commitment to one another to pray for each other and to help one another guard your hearts. Commit to listen when your friend tells you that there is something you are watching, listening to, or doing that she feels may hurt your relationship with God.

Choose to let this friend see behind your mask and share in your good times and bad. In other words, be willing to get the hidden stuff out. James 5:16 tells us to confess our sins to each other and pray for each other so that we may be healed. When we confess our sins, the devil can't trouble us with them anymore. Find a friend to be accountable to right away.

Write down the name of someone to whom you could be accountable. _____

3. Stay open before God.

Tell God everything! Lay your struggles out for Him to see. He sees them anyway. Ask Him for help every time you struggle with something. Ask Him to help you to examine your motives and attitudes so that your heart will stay pure and your life will be a true reflection of a heart wholly devoted to God.

4. Fill your mind with God's truth.

The Word of God is the truth of God. Read it daily, and allow it to transform your heart and mind. When we fail to read the Bible, we often forget who God says we really are ("more than conquerors," for example) and become easy targets for Satan's fiery darts of doubt and discouragement. (See Rom. 8:37.)

Decide right now when and where you will read the Bible each day. Write your commitment down.

I will read my Bible at _____ o'clock each day for _____ minutes/hours.

I will read my Bible (example: in my room, in the kitchen):

_____.

Remember, if you miss a day or the time, don't become discouraged. Just read it later in the day or evening, and begin again the next day. The important thing is to make it a part of your lifestyle to read something from the Word every day.

5. Examine your relationships/friendships.

Proverbs 13:20 says, "He who walks with the wise will grow wise, but a companion of fools suffers harm." Who are your closest friends? Do these people help you to live wholly devoted to God? If not, it is time to pray and ask God to give you some new friends.

You will look and act like the people you spend the most time with. If you want to live a pure life, then you need to spend time with friends who desire the same thing. Breaking away from old friends can be hard, but Jesus will help you to stay strong as you focus on Him and His Word. Believe me, you aren't helping your friends if you aren't really showing them who God is and what He is like. Don't fool yourself.

217

Reflections

Renewing a Promise

As the rain continues to pour and I continue to reflect, I find myself playing with the silver purity ring that I wear on the ring finger of my left hand. The words Wholly Devoted *are inscribed on the band, serving to remind me of my promise to God. Quietly, I renew that promise in my heart.*

A promise to serve God with all your heart, soul, mind, and strength is a promise that must be renewed each day. Make a new promise to Him right now. Renew the promise you made yesterday. Choose to be wholly devoted to Him.

Remember, a choice to be wholly devoted is a choice for God's best in your life.

Endnotes

The Journey

The Heart of the Father

[1] This section contains the author's paraphrased narrative of part of Ezekiel 16, in which the Lord spoke to the prophet Ezekiel allegorically about Jerusalem.

The Free Gift, Part 1

[1] "Just As I Am, Without One Plea," words by Charlotte Elliott, 1835; music by William B. Bradley, *Mendelssohn's Collection or Third Book of Psalmody*, (New York: 1894), available from <http://www.cyberhymnal.org/htm/j/u/justasam.htm>.

The Free Gift, Part 2

[1] *Webster's New World Dictionary of the American Language* (New York, New York: Warner Books, 1983), s.v. "mercy."

Wanted: A Forever Friend

[1] James E. Strong, "Hebrew and Chaldee Dictionary" in *Strong's Exhaustive Concordance of the Bible* (Nashville: Abingdon, 1890), p. 29, entry #1692, s.v. "clave," Ruth 1:14.

Someday My Prince Will Come

[1] "September 22nd Devotional," from *My Utmost for His Highest,* by Oswald Chambers (Uhrichsville, Ohio: Barbour and Company), p. 266.

Happily Ever After

[1] This is an excerpt from *He's Looking for a Bride* by Paige Chavoustie, a speaker and also a teacher in youth and children's ministries. Her Web site is <http.www.inhishands.org>. Used by permission.

Choices of the Heart, Part 1

[1] *Merriam-Webster OnLine Dictionary,* copyright © 2002, s.v. "choice," available from <http://www.m-w.com>.

Dare To Dream God's Dream for Your Life, Part 2

[1] Written by contributing author Rebecca Simmons.

Excellence: God's Standard

[1] Based on a definition from W.E. Vine, *An Expository Dictionary of New Testament Words* (Old Tappan, New Jersey: Fleming H. Revell Company, 1966), p. 55 S.V. "EXCEL, EXCELLENCY, EXCELLENT, 4. DIAPHERO."

Wholly Devoted, Part 1—Staying Pure

[1] Based on a definition from Merriam-Webster, s.v. "pure."

Prayer of Salvation

God loves you—no matter who you are, no matter what your past. God loves you so much that He gave His one and only begotten Son for you. The Bible tells us that "...whoever believes in him shall not perish but have eternal life" (John 3:16 NIV). Jesus laid down His life and rose again so that we could spend eternity with Him in heaven and experience His absolute best on earth. If you would like to receive Jesus into your life, say the following prayer out loud and mean it from your heart.

Heavenly Father, I come to You admitting that I am a sinner. Right now, I choose to turn away from sin, and I ask You to cleanse me of all unrighteousness. I believe that Your Son, Jesus, died on the cross to take away my sins. I also believe that He rose again from the dead so that I might be forgiven of my sins and made righteous through faith in Him. I call upon the name of Jesus Christ to be the Savior and Lord of my life. Jesus, I choose to follow You and ask that You fill me with the power of the Holy Spirit. I declare that right now I am a child of God. I am free from sin and full of the righteousness of God. I am saved in Jesus' name. Amen.

If you prayed this prayer to receive Jesus Christ as your Savior for the first time, please contact us on the Web at **www.harrisonhouse.com** to receive a free book.

Or you may write to us at

Harrison House

P.O. Box 35035

Tulsa, Oklahoma 74153

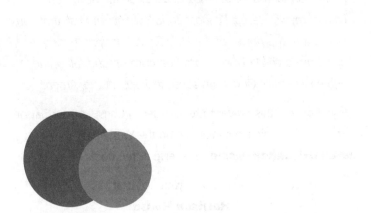

Daughters of Heaven Ministries

*Inspiring young women to seek
and know the heart of God,
discovering intimacy for life!*

Daughters of Heaven Ministries Inc., is a ministry designed for young women, junior high through college age. We have been holding conferences since 1995 and producing Bible studies since 1997. It has been exciting to see hundreds of girls respond to our message with life-changing results.

Devoted to Purity

Our conferences are designed to empower young women with a new, fresh vision of holiness and consecration to God. Our desire is to see the Spirit of God move across this "ready" generation, to turn the tide from apathy to intimacy, from deception to discernment, from destruction to restoration. Young women can live confidently by raising their standards, living lives devoted to purity, and by breaking free from the seductive chains and degrading compromises this world has to offer. It is paramount that young women discover God's vision for them. His desire is for them to lead holy, pure, devoted lives—lives which will bring them freedom, happiness, and true contentment.

> Who may ascend the hill of the Lord? Who may stand in his holy place?
>
> He who has clean hands and a pure heart, who does not lift up his soul to an idol or swear by what is false.
>
> He will receive blessing from the Lord and vindication from God his Savior.
>
> Such is the generation of those who seek him, who see your face, O God of Jacob.
>
> Psalm 24:3-6

Desiring His Presence

Seduced by their need for love and acceptance, many young women seek refuge in dangerous, unfamiliar places. Our society's perception of the truth warps the mind and cloaks the eyes from the true hunger of the heart—to live free from bondage; young women need to be empowered with God's Word and walk daily in His Presence.

God's Presence is real! Young women are seeking truth and fulfillment. We have answers! We seek to empower young women by equipping them with spiritual and tangible tools from the Word of God that will lead to a victorious, confident Christian walk. With His help, it is possible to walk through life focused and filled with the fire of God.

> Blessed are those who hunger and thirst for righteousness for they shall be filled.
> Blessed are the pure in heart, for they shall see God.
>
> Matthew 5:6,8

> For you created my innermost being; you knit me together in my mother's womb.
> I praise you because I am fearfully and wonderfully made; your works are wonderful, I know that full well.
>
> Psalm 139:13,14

Dedicated to His Purpose

God cherishes His daughters! God's unconditional love and acceptance is humbling and life-changing. We desire to instill God's purpose for living in the hearts of His "fearfully and wonderfully made" creations. God's Word reveals to us the Big Picture, and we are snapshots He uses along the way. He has a unique and divine role for each of us to play. Our conferences, Bible studies, and devotionals will help young women discover their own unique gifts, talents, and strengths that God Himself placed within them, helping them make confident, "on-purpose" choices. With God-given purpose, young women will profoundly mark their generation for Christ.

> Your eyes saw my unformed body. All the days ordained for me
> were written in your book before one of them came to be.
>
> Psalm 139:16

Conferences

Each Daughters of Heaven Conference is thoughtfully and carefully designed to bring relevant, fresh, and timely messages to young women. While the atmosphere is upbeat and lively, the information we provide is vital in equipping them to reach out, break through, and take a stand to live lives of victory in Christ!

Main session speakers both challenge and encourage the hearts of girls, helping to prepare them in becoming all that God has intended them to be. Additionally, each conference offers several breakout sessions; we call them "chatrooms," where the girls can get more in-depth, topic-specific teachings on issues they face in society today.

Topics can range anywhere from experiencing meaningful friendships, discovering your unique gifts and talents, to overcoming abuse or divorce.

Throughout all the Daughters of Heaven Conferences, one thing has remained the same: It is a life-changing experience for all who attend.

Event Speakers

Daughters of Heaven Conference speakers are dedicated to equipping and empowering young women everywhere to live lives devoted to purity and purpose. They are sure to bring a timely message to your event that will challenge and encourage all who attend.

About the Author

Suzanne Rentz is the founder and president of Daughters of Heaven Ministries (www.daughtersofheaven.org). Daughters of Heaven is dedicated to inspiring and equipping young women to seek and know the heart of God. Suzanne has been the keynote speaker for the Daughters of Heaven conferences as well as other conferences and women's meetings around the country. She has spoken to the youth at Summer Blitz, Kenneth Hagin's Camp Meeting in Tulsa, Oklahoma, conducted sessions at many Assemblies of God Church Camps, taught Bible studies, and instructed leaders at the Northern California Assemblies of God Leadership Summit.

As a young child growing up in Eureka, California, Suzanne had a deep love for God and a dream to one day stand before women and share the message of His love and acceptance. It was nearly twenty years before that dream became a reality, but in 1991 Suzanne discovered the joy of following the desires of her heart.

That year, in San Jose, California, more than 180 girls attended the first Daughters of Heaven conference—a weekend designed specifically for them. Witnessing the life-changing presence of God wash over the girls as they discovered His great love, forgiveness, and restoration profoundly impacted Suzanne. It was out of this humble beginning that Daughters of Heaven Ministries was birthed. Since then, several D.O.H. conferences have been held throughout the United States and hundreds of young women have been encouraged with life-changing results.

Suzanne's true passion is that young women discover God's love and acceptance, receive a revelation that they are created in His image, and uncover His incredible plan for their lives. Suzanne communicates a strong, clean message from her heart that is crucial for this generation: if young women truly understand their value and incredible worth to their heavenly Father, they can live a life devoted to purity in an ungodly world. With God's keeping and restoring power, regardless of their situation, any young woman can become a woman of virtue and integrity. Offering them hope, she explains that it is never too late to discover a new, fresh level of intimacy with God.

Suzanne says that her best friend and most significant partner in life is her husband, Mark. He is currently serving as an associate pastor at River City Community Church in Sacramento, California, and is an anointed worship leader and gifted speaker. Mark and Suzanne have also taught together at several of the conferences. They reside in Sacramento, California, along with their three fun-loving, adventurous boys: Luke, Andrew ,and Elijah, and their very own little *daughter from heaven,* Gabriella Elizabeth.

To contact Daughters of Heaven Ministries
or Suzanne Rentz,
please write to:

8319 Cedar Crest Way
Sacramento, CA 95826
(916) 381-3872
www.daughtersofheaven.org

*Please include your prayer requests
and comments when you write.*

About the
Contributing Authors

Erin Zonio

Erin earned her B.A. in general ministries at Bethany College in Santa Cruz, California. She spent a summer in Costa Rica while attending language school, then returned to her home church to serve as a children's ministry intern and later a children's pastor. Her husband, Henry, is currently a children's pastor in Corvallis, Oregon. While her focus is taking care of their two young children, she also enjoys ministering with her husband. She can be contacted by e-mail at erinez@juno.com.

Rebecca Simmons

Rebecca is the founder of Imprint Children's Ministries, specializing in children's evangelism through ventriloquism, puppetry, gospel illusions, Bible stories, object lessons, music, and drama. She is also an accomplished speaker who has experience establishing and growing effective Christian children's programs.

Susanna Aughtman

Susanna graduated from Bethany College, in Santa Cruz, California, in 1994, earning a B.A. in social science with an emphasis in psychology and early childhood education. She pursued a career in early childhood development and started her own interior decorating business before leaving to become a full-time mom. She enjoys writing poetry and traveling abroad.

LaFaye Tapper

LaFaye has shared her husband's ministry to families and youth for the past nineteen years as a wife, mother, teacher, role model, and mentor. LaFaye and her husband, E.T., are presently serving as family life pastors at Marysville Assembly of God, Marysville, Washington. They reside in Arlington, Washington, with their five children.

Kim Clements

Kim is a junior high school language arts teacher in Phoenix, Arizona. She is married to Tim Clements, who is the pastor of Phoenix Calvary Temple. They have two sons, Mychal and Taylor.

Vicky Olsen

Vicky travels nationally as a Christian conference speaker and a speaker for CLASServices, founded by her friend and mentor, Florence Littauer. Vicky also writes a bimonthly column for *Woman's Touch* magazine entitled "Up Close & Personal" and often ministers together with her husband, Rick. They reside in Leavenworth, Kansas, with their eleven-month-old daughter, Abby Rose.

Judy Rentz

Judy and her husband, Eddie, have devoted their ministry to youth and youth leaders. They most recently served the Assemblies of God as the National Youth Ministries Director and the District Youth Ministries Director (Northern California/Nevada). They currently pastor River City Community Church in Sacramento, California where Judy also teaches fourth grade. Judy's most fulfilling role is being a mother to her three treasures—Jordyn, Jessica, and Jonathan.

Tanya Devoll

Tanya is an ordained minister with the Assemblies of God. She and her husband, Jeff, were youth pastors for six years before starting their current ministry. Now they are Youth Alive directors for the Northern California/Nevada District of the Assemblies of God. They help churches, students, communities, and adults effectively reach their local junior high and high school campuses for Christ.

Rebecca Harrison

Rebecca and her husband, Wayne, attend the Gathering Place, a church in Folsom, California. She is the mother of four children, is very active in women's ministries, and enjoys leading Bible studies at her church. Rebecca communicates her hunger for studying the Word of God through her writing and teaching style.

Jennifer Davis

Jennifer is an ordained minister with the Assemblies of God and has been in full-time ministry since 1991. She is currently serving alongside her husband, Dwight, as the associate pastor of student ministries at Valley Christian Center in Dublin, California. She says that she has a passion for equipping the saints to live purposeful lives for Christ.

Sarah King

Sarah attends Freedom Christian Center in Manteca, California, where she and her husband, Brandon, are actively involved in music and children's ministries. Sarah and Brandon have been married for six years and have three children—Ryan, Isaac, and Maddison.

Shereen Christian

Shereen is a speaker as well as the promotions director for Daughters of Heaven Ministries. Shereen and her husband, Gary, serve faithfully at New Life Community Church in Fair Oaks, California. They reside in Rocklin, California, with their two daughters, Jessica Sara and Jordyn Elizabeth.

Delia Todd

Delia works alongside Michael, her husband of four years, who is the associate/youth pastor at Calvary Assembly in Milpitas, California. Their vision and passion is to see teens won for Christ, build their relationship with Jesus, and then be sent to do His work. They currently reside in San Jose, California.

Kathy Holt

Kathy is a graduate of Bethany Bible College in Scotts Valley, California, and she is currently teaching fourth grade. She is married to Christopher, who is an associate pastor at River City Community Church in Sacramento, California, and she is the mother of four. Her passion is worshiping and knowing Christ more intimately.

Yolanda Benjamin

Yolanda is currently working alongside her husband, Darwin, who is an evangelist and associate pastor. They are well-known for their testimony, which has been aired on the 700 Club several times. They live in Stockton, California, with their five children.

Lisa Spears

Lisa and her husband, Jason, are currently on staff at First Assembly of God in Griffin, Georgia, where they are directors of the school of ministry called South Atlanta Master's Commission. She also leads a divorce recovery program for children and mentors young girls. Lisa and Jason live in Griffin, Georgia, with their daughter, Brooklen.

www.harrisonhouse.com

Fast. Easy. Convenient!

◆ New Book Information
◆ Look Inside the Book
◆ Press Releases
◆ Bestsellers
◆ Free E-News
◆ Author Biographies

◆ Upcoming Books
◆ Share Your Testimony
◆ Online Product Availability
◆ Product Specials
◆ Order Online

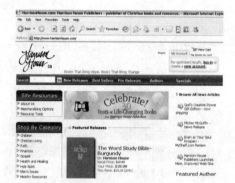

For the latest in book news and author information, please visit us on the Web at www.harrisonhouse.com. Get up-to-date pictures and details on all our powerful and life-changing products. Sign up for our e-mail newsletter, *Friends of the House,* and receive free monthly information on our authors and products including testimonials, author announcements, and more!

Harrison House—
Books That Bring Hope, Books That Bring Change

The Harrison House Vision

Proclaiming the truth and the power
Of the Gospel of Jesus Christ
With excellence;

Challenging Christians to
Live victoriously,
Grow spiritually,
Know God intimately.